BEETHOVEN
AN EXTRAORDINARY LIFE

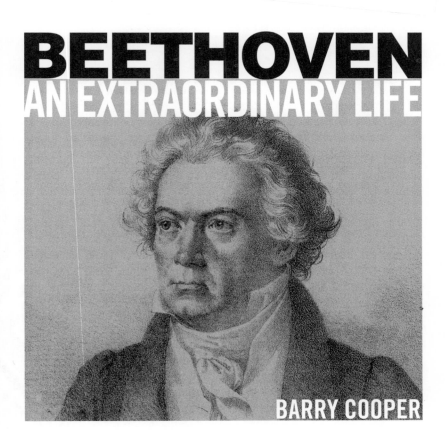

BARRY COOPER

ABRSM

MIX
Paper from
responsible sources
FSC™ C109619
FSC
www.fsc.org

First published in 2013 by ABRSM Publishing Ltd, a wholly owned subsidiary of ABRSM, 24 Portland Place, London W1B 1LU, United Kingdom

© 2013 by The Associated Board of the Royal Schools of Music

ISBN 978 1 84849 489 3
AB 3704

A CIP catalogue for this book is available from The British Library.
Design and formatting by www.9thplanetdesign.com
Typeset by Hope Services (Abingdon) Ltd, England
Printed in England by Halstan & Co. Ltd, Amersham, Bucks

Acknowledgements

Translations

Barry Cooper's translation of the Heiligenstadt Testament (pp. 57–60) is based on the version that appears in *The Beethoven Compendium* by permission of Thames & Hudson Ltd.

Barry Cooper's translation of Beethoven's letter to the 'Immortal Beloved' (pp. 86–87) is partly based on the version by Virginia Beahrs that appears in *The Beethoven Newsletter*, Vol. 5 No. 2 (1990), and is used by permission of the American Beethoven Society and San Jose State University.

We are grateful to the following for the permission to reproduce photographs:

Front cover

Lithograph of Beethoven by Josef Kriehuber, based on a bust by Anton Dietrich and a drawing by Josef Decker. Frontispiece to the first biography of Beethoven, by Johann Schlosser, who described this picture of Beethoven as 'the best among all that have been created'. By permission of the Beethoven-Haus, Bonn.

Beethoven's signature from a letter to Franz Brentano, 12 November 1821. By permission of the Beethoven-Haus, Bonn.

Detail from the autograph score of the Kyrie from Beethoven's *Missa solemnis*.
© bpk-Berlin/Staatsbibliothek zu Berlin.

Inside pages

1. Bust of Beethoven by Franz Klein, based on a life mask from 1812. By permission of the Beethoven-Haus, Bonn.
2. Archduke Rudolph by Johann Baptist Lampi the Younger *c*.1825. © Wien Museum.
3. Sketch leaf of 1796. © The Board of The British Library ('Kafka' Miscellany, Add. MS 29801, f. 71r).
4. Page from Beethoven's pocket sketchbook of summer 1825. © The Board of The British Library (Egerton MS 2795, f. 11r).
5. Score sketch of WoO 62. By permission of the Beethoven-Haus, Bonn (NE 101, f. 1r).
6. Page from Beethoven's sketchbook of 1804–5. © bpk-Berlin/Staatsbibliothek zu Berlin. (Mendelssohn 15, p. 192).
7. Beginning of the cadenza for the first movement of Beethoven's Piano Concerto No. 1 in C. By permission of the Beethoven-Haus, Bonn, Collection H. C. Bodmer (Mh, 11, p. 1).
8. *Missa solemnis* autograph. © bpk-Berlin/ Staatsbibliothek zu Berlin. (Mus. ms. autogr. Beethoven 1, f. 25r)
9. The Kohlmarkt in Vienna. © Wien Museum.
10. Miniature portrait of Beethoven painted in 1802 by Christian Horneman. By permission of the Beethoven-Haus, Bonn, Collection H. C. Bodmer.
11. Prince Karl Lichnowsky painted by an unknown artist. By permission of the Beethoven-Haus, Bonn.
12. The Burgtheater painted by an unknown artist. © Wien Museum.
13. The village of Heiligenstadt painted by Raulino. © Wien Museum.
14. First page of Beethoven's Heiligenstadt Testament of October 1802. By permission of the Staats- und Universitätsbibliothek, Hamburg.
15. A selection of Beethoven's ear-trumpets. By permission of the Beethoven-Haus, Bonn.
16. Antonie Brentano painted by Joseph Stieler. By permission of the Brentano-Haus, Oestrich-Winkel.
17. Final page of the 'Immortal Beloved' letter. © bpk-Berlin/Staatsbibliothek zu Berlin.
18. Engraving by V. R. Grüner of a scene from *Fidelio*. © Wien Museum.
19. Unsigned miniature of Beethoven's nephew Karl. © Wien Museum.
20. Beethoven's Erard piano. By permission of the Oberösterreichisches Landesmuseum, Linz.
21. Portrait of Beethoven in 1820 by Joseph Stieler. By permission of the Beethoven-Haus, Bonn (Landon No. 207).
22. Page from one of Beethoven's conversation books. Photograph © bpk-Berlin/Staats-bibliothek zu Berlin (book no. 83, f. 15v).
23. Beethoven's funeral procession painted by Franz Stöber. By permission of the Beethoven-Haus, Bonn.
24. The first two sides of Beethoven's appeal memorandum. By permission of the Beethoven-Haus, Bonn, Collection H. C. Bodmer (Bodmer HBC Br 1).

For Susan, who has shown such great interest

Contents

Preface

This book is intended to provide a compact summary of the main events in Beethoven's extraordinary life. Its structure is partly modelled on other books in the series by Davitt Moroney (Bach), Julian Rushton (Mozart), and J. P. E. Harper-Scott (Elgar), and it is intended for music-lovers in general, avoiding technical detail as far as possible. Those wishing to read a fuller and more technical account of Beethoven's life and works are recommended to consult my *Beethoven* in the Master Musicians series.[1] This provides amplification and bibliographical references for much of the information found in the present study, and it was based on a thorough reassessment of the reliability of documents and anecdotes relating to Beethoven. The most outstanding early biographer of Beethoven was Alexander Wheelock Thayer, whose researches have provided an important foundation for all subsequent biographies including the present one.[2] The basis for any unreferenced biographical details given here can almost always be traced through either my Master Musicians book or Thayer, who was meticulous in sifting fact from fiction and largely avoided the inaccuracies found in many other early accounts. Some of the more glaring fallacies and distortions present in these accounts have been gathered together in the final chapter of the present book, 'Myths about Beethoven'.

The importance of reliable documents as a basis for any biography is reflected in the fact that each of the five main chronological chapters is followed by an 'inter-chapter' (to borrow Rushton's phrase) that focuses on one or more documents written by Beethoven himself. These documents have been deliberately chosen so as to illuminate five very different aspects of his life. In order to understand them better, however, it is important to appreciate the context in which he worked, inasmuch as it

---

[1] Barry Cooper, *Beethoven* (Oxford: Oxford University Press, 2000; 2nd edn, New York, 2008).
[2] Thayer's work, which was still unfinished at his death, has been published in various different versions, most notably in that by Elliot Forbes, abbreviated here as TF; there is also a fuller German version edited by Hermann Deiters and Hugo Riemann (TDR; for a full list of abbreviations used, see the Bibliography).

affected his life. Consequently the Introduction sets out the framework in which he had to operate in order to make a living as a composer.

I should like to thank Robin Barry and Leslie East for suggesting this project, and also all those who have presented me with ideas or information over the years, thereby indirectly contributing to the writing of the book. These include especially Theodore Albrecht, Otto Biba, Sieghard Brandenburg, Clive Brown, Anne-Louise Coldicott, Peter Davies, Jonathan Del Mar, Tia DeNora, William Drabkin, Owen Jander, David Wyn Jones, Susan Kagan, Joseph Kerman, William Kinderman, Lewis Lockwood, Nicholas Marston, William Meredith, Julia Moore, Maynard Solomon, Glenn Stanley, Marie-Elisabeth Tellenbach, Alan Tyson, Jos van der Zanden, and Petra Weber-Bockholdt. I should also like to thank all the libraries and institutions that have been so helpful in providing me with materials which have contributed to this biography, in particular the Beethoven-Archiv, Bonn; the Ira F. Brilliant Center for Beethoven Studies, San Jose; the Gesellschaft der Musikfreunde, Vienna; the Musikabteilung of the Staatsbibliothek zu Berlin, Preussischer Kulturbesitz; the British Library, London; and the Bibliothèque Nationale, Paris. Finally I must thank particularly my wife Susan for all her support and interest throughout the time I have been studying Beethoven's life and works.

Barry Cooper
University of Manchester

INTRODUCTION:
Patrons and Publishers

Earning a living

Composers in Beethoven's day, as now, hardly ever made a living purely through selling new compositions to eager buyers. In other respects, however, the life of a composer then was very different from that of one today, and to understand how someone such as Beethoven could flourish in the late eighteenth and early nineteenth centuries it is essential to have some awareness of the political and social background to his life. At that time Germany, where he was born and spent his youth, was not a united country but a loose association of semi-autonomous states mostly bound together within the so-called Holy Roman Empire, which was neither holy nor Roman and arguably not even an empire. The overall rulers were the Habsburg dynasty, who resided in Vienna, and they also ruled Austria, which occupied a much larger area than today, as well as the kingdom of Hungary. Each of the states had its own local ruler and court, and it was up to the ruler to decide how much patronage was allocated to different art forms. As it happened, many of these rulers showed much partiality to music, with the result that court orchestras and sometimes opera flourished in many places in German-speaking countries, with considerable rivalry between them. Bach had served as music director at the court at Cöthen for a time, and the court at Mannheim became particularly celebrated for its outstanding instrumental music around the middle of the eighteenth century.

Another such court could be found in Bonn, on the River Rhine in north-west Germany, where Beethoven was born in 1770. At that time Bonn was a small town of barely 10,000 inhabitants, but it had long boasted a thriving musical life, due to the role of the local ruler the Elector of Cologne, who was also Archbishop of Cologne but traditionally resided in nearby Bonn. His position was both ecclesiastical and political, in that he

1

and other electors were entitled to elect, at least notionally, the Holy Roman Emperor, and he wielded considerable power and influence. Although much of north Germany at that time was Protestant, the area around Bonn and Cologne remained Catholic at the time of the Reformation and has continued to do so ever since. The amount of music-making at the Bonn court varied over the years, depending partly on finances and partly on the preferences of each elector, but at the time of Beethoven's birth it included a good number of professional musicians.[1]

As Beethoven grew up and displayed musical talent he naturally became absorbed into the musical life of the Bonn court and was soon being employed officially by the elector, Maximilian Friedrich. Thus his position there was in some ways similar to Haydn's under Prince Esterházy at Eisenstadt, in that a single main patron provided for his needs, in return for his performing whatever musical tasks he was called upon to do, although Beethoven held a far more junior position than Haydn and was not in any way responsible for running the musical establishment. Apart from his employment by the Elector of Cologne, Beethoven was also at times supported by less official patrons, notably Count Waldstein. Composition was largely a sideline at this stage, though he was allowed plenty of spare time to engage in it.

When Beethoven moved to Vienna in 1792, however, he found himself in a very different environment. Vienna was not merely the capital of the Habsburg Empire and the German-speaking world but was the largest German-speaking city, with a population of around 200,000. It was therefore the centre of much musical activity, sponsored by several rich noblemen who were great music-lovers, and supported by many other enthusiasts. The city was also home to a number of composers, all of whom needed to make a living. Most of them were excellent players on at least one instrument, and were able to use their compositions as the basis for performances that could be sufficiently attractive to paying audiences or supporting sponsors to ensure a reasonable standard of living. Thus much of their income would often come from a combination of composition and performance, whether in the theatre, the concert hall, the church, or the private salon, and whether as soloist, ensemble player, or overall music director. They might also perform works written by other composers, but the attraction of a new work specially written for an occasion, at a time when most music being performed was less than 20 years old, was most likely to draw in a substantial audience and with it the necessary income.

In this environment Beethoven was no longer employed by a single patron as before, and was effectively a freelance musician (apart from some residual payments from the Elector of Cologne, which ceased after

---

[1] Details of the Bonn court and its musical establishment are given in TF, especially pp. 3–40.

1. *Bust of Beethoven. Since it is based on a life mask made in 1812, its proportions are accurate, though it does not convey the facial expression as well as some portraits.*

about a year). Thereafter, in the absence of any appointment in theatre, church, or court, he had to earn a living by impressing patrons sufficiently for them to want to sponsor him, and it is a mark of his extraordinary ability that he was able to do this so successfully during the 1790s, although conversely, without some extremely rich and generous music-loving patrons he would never have been able to flourish in Vienna at that time.[2] His first major patron was Prince Karl Lichnowsky, but soon he had gained several more, among whom the most generous was Prince Franz von Lobkowitz. Beethoven was allowed to live in Lichnowsky's house in Vienna shortly after his arrival, and later he was allowed to perform some of his most recent compositions, including the *Eroica* Symphony, in Lobkowitz's palace.

At first Beethoven was sponsored mainly as a performer, since he had already developed remarkable skill as a pianist. Solo recitals were unknown in those days, but numerous musical soirées (and some matinees) were held by certain noblemen, where he could perform for appropriate reward. In 1796 Johann Schönfeld published a book in which he listed no

---

[2] This point is made very emphatically in Tia DeNora, *Beethoven and the Construction of Genius: Musical Politics in Vienna, 1792–1803* (Berkeley: University of California Press, 1995).

fewer than twenty-four individuals who from time to time gave large or small concerts at their houses.[3] Although such events left little documentation, Lichnowsky held a concert every Friday, and several of Beethoven's new compositions were first performed at these, with Beethoven himself playing the piano either solo or with accompaniment. He also often extemporized on the piano at these events – a skill at which he greatly excelled – since extemporization (or improvisation, as it is now generally called) was extremely common on such occasions. Thus he was producing what might be described as 'instant compositions' on a regular basis. Ideas from some of these may later have been worked into actual compositions, but otherwise they are totally lost. Nevertheless, composing activity of this kind not only encouraged patrons to continue supporting him, but also enabled him to build a reputation that would provide a solid foundation for future development, as well as offering opportunities for him to experiment with new ideas for written-out compositions.

Once Beethoven had established himself as a composer, by writing works to be performed at these soirées, patrons began commissioning new works for a fee. The patron could choose the genre, but Beethoven alone would always decide on the musical style. The system for such commissions was explained succinctly by his brother Carl in a letter of 5 December 1802, which refers to the works that had been commissioned from Beethoven during the previous ten years:

> These pieces were mostly commissioned by amateurs under the following agreement: he who wants a piece pays a specified sum for its exclusive possession for half or a whole year, or even longer, and undertakes not to give the manuscript to <u>anybody</u>; <u>after</u> <u>this period</u>, the composer is free to do what he wishes with it.[4]

Thus the curious pattern of Beethoven's early Viennese works, with a mixture of piano sonatas, violin sonatas, string trios, string quartets, and other chamber works produced singly or in groups in a somewhat random order, was determined largely by a succession of private patrons rather than by Beethoven himself. Theoretically he could of course refuse commissions – it seems he was reluctant to embark on a set of string quartets until he felt sufficiently confident – but mostly he went along with what was requested, and he could not anyway afford to refuse generous commissions. Far from finding the system stultifying or restricting, however, as a lesser composer might have done, he used it to develop a highly original style in which every work differed markedly

---

[3] Elaine Sisman, ed., *Haydn and his World* (Princeton, NJ: Princeton University Press, 1997), pp. 318–19.
[4] Alb-10; BB-119.

from every previous one, while still being recognizably within a personal style that differed from those of all other composers. This was no mean achievement.

It was therefore private patrons – individual members of the aristocracy – who provided the bulk of Beethoven's income up to the early 1800s. Besides Lichnowsky and Lobkowitz, names that are known include Count Moritz Fries, Baron Peter von Braun, Count Johann Georg von Browne, Prince Joseph zu Schwarzenberg, Countess Josephine Clary, Count Andreas Razumovsky, and even Empress Maria Theresia, wife of the ruling monarch, Emperor Franz. The King of Prussia, Friedrich Wilhelm II, also supported Beethoven during the composer's visit to Berlin in 1796. In later years Beethoven's patrons included Archduke Rudolph of Austria (a particular friend and generous patron), Countess Marie Erdödy, Baron Ignaz von Gleichenstein, and his very last patron, Prince Nikolas Galitzin of St Petersburg, who commissioned three of the late quartets. The most remarkable piece of sponsorship, however, came with a unique agreement by three noblemen in 1809 – Prince Lobkowitz, Archduke Rudolph, and Prince Ferdinand Kinsky – to provide Beethoven with a lifelong annuity that was intended to be sufficient to provide for his everyday needs. Only a composer of exceptional merit could ever have received such a generous allowance, and only Beethoven is known to have been the recipient of any such scheme. It enabled him, in theory at least, to compose whatever he wanted, for the rest of his life, untroubled by financial worries. Although the value of the annuity was quickly eroded by inflation, it remained an important source of income for him.

Public performances

Beethoven's other methods of receiving remuneration for composition were less reliable. He never held a church position in Vienna, even though he had been court organist in Bonn, and so he could not rely on a limited but steady income such as had been received by so many earlier church composers, including Monteverdi, Purcell, Bach, and his own teacher Albrechtsberger. Beethoven did do some piano teaching of his own, but rather unwillingly except as a favour to a select few, and the only composition pupil he ever took on was Archduke Rudolph, whom he could not easily have refused after Rudolph had made such a generous contribution to his annuity.

Another possibility for making a living from composition came from the theatre, where several composers were active in Vienna, either at one of the two court theatres (the Burgtheater and the Kärntnerthortheater) or at some private establishment, of which the most important was the Theater an der Wien. However, Beethoven had not composed any operas while in Bonn (perhaps surprisingly, since he had played the viola in many that had been staged there), and when considering the possibility of

2. Archduke Rudolph (1788–1831), in a painting by Johann Baptist Lampi the Younger, c.1825. A close friend and supporter of Beethoven, and his only composition pupil, Rudolph received numerous dedications, including the 'Archduke' Trio and the Missa solemnis.

writing an opera he was more choosy than most about his libretti. Thus for a long time he did not attempt opera. Perhaps he was again reluctant, as with the string quartet, to embark on a major genre until he felt sufficiently confident. He did write two ballets – one commissioned by Count Waldstein in Bonn and one by the ballet-master Salvatore Viganò at the Burgtheater in 1801 (at least one assumes there was a commission, though documentation is lacking) – but he received no commissions for any further works in this field. When he did finally obtain a theatre position, in 1803 at the Theater an der Wien, where he lodged for a time, he gave up on the first opera he began – *Vestas Feuer* (The Vestal Fire) – because of the poor quality of the libretto, and then took a further two years to complete his one fully fledged opera, *Leonore* or *Fidelio* (there is some confusion about its title: today the early versions are known as *Leonore* and the final version of 1814 as *Fidelio*, but in 1805 the work was already called *Fidelio* in correspondence and on the advertisement for the premiere). Such lengthy gestation for a single opera was unusual with his contemporaries, and was the result of a variety of factors, including his determination to succeed in producing something outstanding in a genre that he had not previously attempted. He then spent several additional months revising the opera in 1806 and again in 1814, when it finally achieved success. Other opera projects were considered and rejected, either because of the subject matter or because the terms offered by the theatre management were insufficiently generous. He eventually began collaboration on a new libretto, *Melusine*, with the renowned Franz Grillparzer, after the poet had visited him with it in May 1823, but death intervened before a note was written. From a financial point of view, Beethoven's greatest theatrical success may therefore have been his two one-act singspiels – *Die Ruinen von Athen* (The Ruins of Athens) and *König Stephan* (King Stephen) – that were commissioned in 1811 for the opening of a new theatre in Pest (now part of Budapest).

Aside from private performances in salons, opportunities for giving public concerts of new instrumental works were limited. There was no concert hall as such in Vienna during Beethoven's lifetime, and for most of the time no regular concert-giving body or concert series. One-off concerts were sometimes given, but these had to take place in either a theatre or some other venue that was less than ideal, such as a ballroom, a large restaurant, or even the open air. Of these possibilities, a theatre was perhaps the best, but theatres were normally reserved for opera or ballet; concerts could normally be given there only during Holy Week, the week before Easter, a time of great solemnity, when opera was forbidden for religious reasons. Composers did, however, occasionally have the opportunity to mount a benefit concert or *Akademie*, either at a theatre or elsewhere. Such concerts were usually longer than modern ones, with a newly written concerto played by the composer often being the outstanding attraction. Composers had to make all the arrangements for such concerts but could take any profit that was made, and these events were sometimes quite lucrative. Beethoven's first two benefit concerts took place in 1800 and 1803, in the Burgtheater and the Theater an der Wien respectively. The takings from the first concert are not recorded, but the profit from the second amounted to 1,800 gulden or florins.[5] Since Haydn had reported in 1793 that Beethoven needed nearly 1,000 florins a year, and it was calculated in 1804 that the basic cost of living for an average unmarried middle-class man (a category into which Beethoven broadly fits) was 967 florins,[6] this one concert on its own enabled Beethoven to live more than comfortably for well over a year. Unfortunately he was unable to repeat this success in most subsequent years, except around 1813–14, when he once again earned some large

---

[5] TDR, vol. 3, p. 385.
[6] Alice M. Hanson, 'Incomes and Outgoings in the Vienna of Beethoven and Schubert', *Music & Letters*, 64 (1983), p. 178.

sums. These allowed him to purchase some bank shares that he was later able to bequeath to his nephew.

Music printing

An additional source of income came from printed publications, which became particularly important for Beethoven towards the end of his life. Music printing as an industry grew enormously during the eighteenth century. Very few of Bach's works were printed before 1800, and many of Haydn's remained in manuscript until long after his death. Mozart fared slightly better, but even then a substantial portion of his output remained unpublished at his death, so that his widow Constanze was later able to sell fifteen parcels of his manuscripts to a publisher.[7] There had been virtually no music publishing in Vienna before 1778, but in that year the Artaria family began issuing music editions there; the business quickly flourished, and by the 1790s several Viennese music publishers were active. As a result, almost all of Beethoven's major works written from that time onwards were published within five years of composition, and some of them rapidly went through several editions, with more than one publisher.

Initially publishers simply bought works that Beethoven had already composed. As there was only a limited concept of copyright, and certainly no international copyright, publishers paid a lump sum for a work, rather than royalties, and they hoped to cover this sum and their printing costs through sales. If they were lucky they could make a handsome profit, but they could equally make a loss, and many publishers were forced into liquidation during Beethoven's lifetime. Beethoven's music quickly became popular after his arrival in Vienna, so that by 1801 he was able to boast: 'For every composition I have six or seven publishers, and even more, if I want to make use of them; people no longer bargain with me, I demand and they pay.'[8] This was not always true, since it depended partly on the genre of the work in question: symphonies were more expensive to print than piano works, and therefore harder for Beethoven to sell. Nevertheless, as his fame spread in Europe, more distant publishers such as Breitkopf & Härtel of Leipzig began enquiring what he might have available for them, and this firm eventually published many of his works, including the Fifth and Sixth Symphonies. Another possibility was to sell the same work simultaneously to two publishers in different countries, usually one English publisher and one German or Austrian. Provided that the two editions appeared about the same time, each publisher would have some copyright protection from piracy within his own country. Thus

---

[7] See Heinz Gärtner, *Constanze Mozart: After the Requiem*, trans. Reinhard G. Pauly (Portland, OR: Amadeus Press, 1991), p. 108.
[8] A-51; BB-65.

Beethoven sometimes received two fees for one work, as Haydn had done previously.

It had long been the custom to distinguish a composer's different instrumental works by giving each an opus number, in order of publication, and this tradition continued with Beethoven, at least in theory. In practice, however, things did not always work out. On a few occasions two different works were allocated the same number, while other numbers were omitted altogether. Most of these anomalies have been ironed out since Beethoven's death, but the result is that the opus number is not always a guide to the order of composition (for example, the Wind Octet, Op. 103, dates from before Op. 1). Several minor works and early works do not have an opus number at all, and are now known by a WoO number (WoO = *Werk ohne Opuszahl* or work without opus number; a few very minor works lack even a WoO number, and for most of these a number allocated by Willy Hess is now used).

Most of the time, publishers were content to print works that had already been written for some other purpose such as a commission, but increasingly they began to commission works themselves during Beethoven's later life. The first significant case known is his three piano sonatas Op. 31, which were commissioned by the Swiss publisher Johann Georg Nägeli in 1802. This commission was followed by a long-running one from the Edinburgh publisher George Thomson, who requested a large number of folksong settings and variations from Beethoven during the period 1809–20. Then at the very end of Beethoven's life, after he had written the three quartets for Prince Galitzin, which publishers eagerly snapped up, these same publishers demanded further quartets from him, and he was happy to complete two more for them before his death in 1827.

Thus from his various sources of income Beethoven was able to earn a decent enough living. He never became rich, unlike Handel or Clementi, and he never tried to do so. His view was that an artist like himself should receive what he needed to live on and let that suffice. Any excess he received was either given away to someone in need or set aside as a legacy for his nephew. What was remarkable was that he was able to devote so much of his life simply to being a composer and selling his compositions. He did so partly through necessity, with increasing deafness limiting performing opportunities. But the fact that his compositions found such a ready market that he could earn enough to live on is one of many indications of his exceptional ability and of the widespread recognition of this ability by his contemporaries. Conversely, the amount of time he was able to devote to composition gave him the opportunity to develop his art to unprecedented levels of sophistication and artistry over many years, and was one reason why he was able to crown his output with such amazing works as the Ninth Symphony, the *Missa solemnis*, and the late quartets.

ONE

THE BONN YEARS (1770–1792)

The Beethoven family

It was the musical life of the court at Bonn that initially attracted Beethoven's grandfather, also called Ludwig (or more often the French form, Louis), to the city in 1733 at the age of 21. Louis had originally lived in the Mechelen district of what is now Belgium, and his ancestors were Flemish (the name Van Beethoven probably indicates that some of them came from a beet farm). He was employed at Bonn first as a court musician and eventually rose to the position of Kapellmeister, or music director, in 1761. Louis's son Johann, born about 1740, showed musical talent too, and joined the musical establishment at court as a tenor, as well as teaching keyboard and violin. He married a young widow, Maria Magdalena Leym or Laym (née Keverich), in 1767, and their first child was born in 1769. This was Ludwig Maria, but he died in infancy, as had Maria's son from her first marriage. It was not until December 1770 that the Beethovens' second son, the composer, was born. He was baptized on 17 December at St Remigius's Church (the church has since been demolished, but another church nearby has taken over its name), and evidence indicates that he was born the previous day, although there is no absolute proof of this.

Beethoven was just over three years old when his grandfather died, but he retained fond memories of him for the rest of his life, and seems to have determined at a very early age to follow in his footsteps as a musician. Beethoven states that he came to love music by the age of four, and we may presume that he began about that time to learn from his father to play the keyboard (initially the clavichord or harpsichord, later the piano). By all accounts his father was a very strict and severe teacher, but this on its own would never have turned Beethoven into a musician: he also displayed exceptional talent. Indeed he made such good progress that he was able to perform in public at the age of seven. On 26 March 1778

Johann van Beethoven presented a concert in Cologne given by two of his pupils: 'Mdlle. Averdonc, court contralto, and his little son of six years. The former will have the honour to contribute various fine arias, the latter various keyboard concertos and trios.'[1] Beethoven's age was given incorrectly, either deliberately or through oversight, and for many years he was unsure of the year of his birth. What is more significant, however, is the large age gap between him and Helene Averdonk (Averdonc), who was a full ten years older than him.[2] Johann was not trying to promote his youngest pupils but just two specially selected for the occasion; and he clearly considered that his son would not suffer by comparison when placed alongside a much older girl. The music Beethoven had learnt for the occasion was also strikingly ambitious. Concertos were not in those days the virtuosic works that they became during his lifetime, but they were still regarded as the most challenging type of instrumental music. The orchestral parts were usually incorporated into the piano part in printed editions at that time, and this may have been what Beethoven played, though he probably had a small string group (perhaps one instrument per part) to support his performance of concertos and trios, and to accompany Averdonk's arias.

Beethoven's mother gave birth to five more children, but only two of them survived infancy: Caspar Carl (1774–1815) and Nikolaus Johann (1776–1848), known as Carl and Johann. Both of them studied music as children, but neither showed any real aptitude and they never developed as musicians, despite the efforts their father may have made. Beethoven himself, however, continued making extraordinarily rapid progress, which was enhanced by the arrival in Bonn in 1779 of a highly talented composer, Christian Gottlob Neefe (1748–98). Neefe was appointed music director of a theatre company that the Elector of Cologne had recently established, and he quickly built up its musical side, mounting performances of several operas and similar stage works in the next few years, including Mozart's *Die Entführung aus dem Serail* (The Abduction from the Seraglio). Neefe was additionally appointed to the post of court organist in 1782, by which time Beethoven was able to act as deputy when he was away.

A second Mozart?

The following year Neefe published a description of musical life in Bonn, in a communication dated 2 March 1783 which was printed in Carl Friedrich Cramer's *Magazin der Musik*. Neefe made no particular effort to single out Beethoven specially, but described the whole range of current musical activity, naming nearly all the musicians and writing extensively on some of them. It was impossible, however, to paint an adequate picture

---

[1] See TF, p. 57.
[2] She was born on 11 Dec. 1760: see TF, p. 24.

without reporting on Beethoven, who had by this time become such a prominent part of the scene, even though he was still only 12. Thus Neefe wrote a full paragraph about him, as follows.

> Louis van Betthoven [sic], son of the above-mentioned tenor, a boy of eleven, and of most promising talent. He plays the keyboard very skilfully and with power, sight-reads very well, and to put it in a nutshell: he plays chiefly *Das wohltemperirte Clavier* of Sebastian Bach, which Herr Neefe put into his hands. Whoever knows this collection of preludes and fugues in all the keys (which one might almost call the *non plus ultra*) will know what that means. Herr Neefe has also, as far as his other duties permit, given him an introduction to thorough-bass. Now he is training him in composition, and for his encouragement has had printed in Mannheim 9 variations for clavier by him on a march. This young genius deserves support so that he can travel. He would surely become a second Wolfgang Amadeus Mozart, if he continued as he has begun.[3]

This announcement shows that Beethoven was already an accomplished keyboard player capable of attempting some of the most difficult music then available: Bach's *Well-Tempered Clavier*. Although this magnificent work was still unpublished, Neefe had studied in Leipzig – Bach's final place of work – from 1769 to 1771 and had presumably acquired one of the many manuscript copies then in circulation. The set of variations that Neefe mentions is Beethoven's earliest known composition, though he may have written and certainly must have extemporized earlier ones. The work is based on a march by Ernst Dressler, and one of its most remarkable features is its key of C minor. Whereas all of Mozart's sixteen sets of keyboard variations, like nearly all contemporary sets, are in major keys, Beethoven uses the minor, suggesting an unusually serious outlook – an outlook that persisted in his later works and was soon being noted by his contemporaries. It is also significant that he subsequently wrote far more works in C minor than in any other minor key, and it is striking that his preference for this key was already evident at such an early stage. More remarkable still, the final variation is in C major, so that the work ends in a blaze of glory after a funereal opening. The aesthetic and emotional relationship between C minor and C major has never been the same since Beethoven, and it is extraordinary that already, at the age of 11, he was able to sense the possibilities inherent in this contrast of keys and to exploit them in an original way, anticipating a change of mode that he

---

[3] Translated from TDR, vol. 1, p. 150.

frequently adopted in later works (notably the Fifth Symphony) and creating a new relationship that has permeated music ever since.

Neefe was absolutely right to describe Beethoven as a 'young genius' and a second Mozart. Mozart had only passed through Bonn once, in 1763, on his way to London, but his achievements were clearly well known to Neefe and his intended readers. The proposal that Beethoven should be allowed to travel suggests that Neefe felt himself to be reaching the limits of what he could teach him. There were several precedents for young Bonn musicians being sponsored by the elector to travel to major musical centres to further their development,[4] and Neefe clearly believed this would be an appropriate course for Beethoven, though they had to wait until 1787 before the proposal was put into effect.

Meanwhile Beethoven continued composing enthusiastically, and by the end of the summer had completed three new piano sonatas (WoO 47). These could of course be played on either harpsichord or clavichord instead, but the appearance of a crescendo at one point, and *ff* at several others, makes both these instruments less suitable than the piano. Beethoven's style is already in evidence right from the outset of No. 1, where sudden off-beat accents are accompanied by energetic, pulsating left-hand figuration, producing an effect that seems uncharacteristic of either Haydn or Mozart, whom Beethoven would have been most likely to imitate. No. 2 is even more abnormal, for it begins with a short slow introduction, a feature not found in any keyboard sonata by Haydn or Mozart, though it is not unusual in Haydn's symphonies. The implication is that Beethoven was already thinking on a loftier scale, with the idea of a symphony lurking at the back of his mind long before he completed such a work. More surprising still, the slow introduction is recalled later in the movement during the sonata-form Allegro, a procedure that seems to have been completely unprecedented. Yet it was such a successful idea that Beethoven himself returned to it several times in later years, as in the *Pathétique* Sonata and some of the late quartets; it was also adopted by other composers, such as Haydn in his 'Drum Roll' Symphony of 1795. Thus, as with the Dressler Variations, Beethoven was generating extraordinary new ideas that were to have far-reaching consequences in later music. Child composers often have original ideas, but rarely such significant ones. The three sonatas were published later in 1783, with a dedication to Elector Maximilian Friedrich.

Shortly after this, Beethoven set off with his mother by boat down the Rhine to visit a relative in Rotterdam, according to the recollections many years later of the Fischer family,[5] in whose house the Beethovens were

---

[4] Summarized in Cooper, *Beethoven*, p. 9 (2nd edn, p. 10).
[5] Gottfried Fischer (1780–1864) pieced together family recollections about Beethoven, especially those of Gottfried's older sister Cäcilia, in the 1830s, and these have been published in Joseph Schmidt-Görg (ed.), *Des Bonner Bäckermeisters Gottfried Fischer Aufzeichnungen über Beethovens Jugend* (Bonn: Beethovenhaus, 1971). The account of the trip to the Netherlands is on pp. 64–7.

living at the time. In Rotterdam Beethoven gave several private performances, and a document discovered in 1965 indicates that he also performed at the royal court in The Hague, some ten miles away, on 23 November 1783. What is most remarkable is the fee he received for this performance: 63 florins. Of the other musicians who took part in the event, the composer Carl Stamitz received 14 florins and the rest of the band only 7 each.[6] Though still only 12 years old, Beethoven was clearly the star attraction of the event, and he must have performed an extended solo – probably a concerto and perhaps an extemporization too – to be awarded such a large fee. Despite the generous size of the fee, however, Beethoven recalled later (according to Fischer) that he thought the Dutch were penny-pinchers, and he determined never to go to the Netherlands again. Other writers of the time paint a similar picture of the Dutch, who charged a fee even for walking along the promenade by the sea near The Hague (which Beethoven may have done while there).[7] It was typical of Beethoven to be irritated about paying out small sums of money for no good reason, as is frequently evident in his later dealings with publishers.

If Beethoven did play a concerto in The Hague, it could well have been one he had composed, and the piano part of such a concerto still survives (WoO 4), with his own annotations and the inscription 'agè [*sic*] de douze ans' (aged 12 years). Considering his uncertainty about his age as a child (he generally thought he was a year younger than he was), we cannot be certain precisely when this concerto was written, and it is more likely to date from the following year (1784). It is, however, the most ambitious and large-scale single work that he is known to have composed around that time, and certainly could have been written for The Hague.

Not long after his return to Bonn, Beethoven petitioned the elector to be granted the position of assistant court organist, having already deputized for Neefe unofficially both as organist and as accompanist at rehearsals of stage works. The appointment was duly made, and thus Beethoven received his first salaried position at the age of only 13. The size of the salary had not actually been determined when the elector died and was promptly replaced by Maximilian Franz. The new elector disbanded the theatre company but retained Neefe as court organist, with Beethoven as his deputy on a salary of 150 florins. Both Beethoven and his father were described in court documents of this time as 'poor', though their supposed poverty has at times been much exaggerated.[8]

With no active theatre company performing operas any more, Beethoven's official duties were light and evidently left him plenty of time for composition. He had by this time published two rondos for piano and

[6] Alb-3.

[7] See Jos van der Zanden, 'Letter to the Editor', *The Beethoven Journal*, 21 (2006), p. 47.

[8] See Maynard Solomon, 'Economic Circumstances of the Beethoven Household in Bonn', *Journal of the American Musicological Society*, 50 (1997), pp. 331–51.

two songs, as well as the variations and three sonatas already mentioned. No further publications ensued until 1791, but among major works of the mid-1780s are the above-mentioned piano concerto in E flat; a triple concerto for flute, bassoon, and piano (Hess 13), of which only a fragment of the slow movement survives; a trio for the same three instruments without orchestral accompaniment; and three impressive quartets for violin, viola, cello, and piano (WoO 36). Though partly modelled on three violin sonatas that Mozart had recently published, these quartets surpass their models in many ways, and the middle one in particular (now known as No. 1) is very striking for its powerful and thoroughly Beethovenian Allegro in the rare key of E flat minor.[9]

Into adolescence

During this period Beethoven was also developing significantly as a person, and the beliefs and attitudes that were to permeate the rest of his life were taking shape. He had already inherited or acquired from his mother, a good and pious woman, a desire to do good and live honourably. His religious beliefs, which centred on a loving heavenly Father rather than great affection for the Church and its traditions, are apparent in his choice of text for one of his earliest songs, 'An einen Säugling' (To an Infant), which he had published in 1784. The text compares an infant's lack of understanding of who is nourishing it to humanity's inability to comprehend the unseen hand of God providing for us. Throughout his life, Beethoven chose his song texts with great care, setting only those whose sentiments he could share. Thus we can be sure that he endorsed the concepts expressed in this poem by Johann von Döring.[10]

Beethoven's love of humanity influenced his political attitudes too, which were reinforced by the intellectual climate of the 1780s. Joseph II, Emperor of Austria from 1780 to 1790, was an enlightened ruler who favoured a much more liberal regime than had prevailed previously, and his ideas were endorsed in Bonn by Maximilian Franz, who was actually his youngest brother. Beethoven's strongly anti-tyrannical views, which were to surface in several later compositions such as *Fidelio* and *Egmont*, took firm root in this fertile intellectual environment. He also developed a strong love of literature about this time. This was not so much through the court or his family as through friends. Particularly important in this regard was the Von Breuning family, which at that time consisted of the widow Helene and her four children, Eleonore, Christoph, Stephan, and Lorenz. Beethoven was introduced to them by a young medical student, Franz Wegeler, when a piano teacher was needed for two of the children.

---

[9] For further discussion of these three quartets, see e.g. Cooper, *Beethoven*, pp. 17–19 (2nd edn, pp. 18–21).
[10] For the full text of the poem with English translation, see Paul Reid, *The Beethoven Song Companion* (Manchester: Manchester University Press, 2007), p. 65.

Wegeler, who later married Eleonore, recorded later, 'Beethoven was soon treated as one of the children in the family and not only did he spend the greatest part of the day there but even many nights.'[11] The family was much more affluent than the Beethoven household, where much of the father's income was spent on alcohol, and was consequently able to lead a much more cultured existence. It was here that Beethoven was introduced to the delights of German and classical literature, and he acquired a lifelong love of the works of Goethe, Homer, and other writers.

He could not have continued to progress in music, however, without the active support of Maximilian Franz. Although the elector's disbanding of the theatre company and halving of Neefe's salary (soon restored) suggest a financially cautious ruler, he was prepared to use his wealth to support deserving causes. Only a year after arriving in Bonn he founded the university that still flourishes there today, and his love of music matched his love of learning in general. He was a capable viola player and singer, and in 1775 Mozart had written his opera *Il rè pastore* for the then archduke's visit to Mozart's home city of Salzburg. The two men met up again in Vienna when Mozart moved there in 1781, and after taking up his position in Bonn the elector returned to Vienna for a brief visit in October 1785. We may surmise that he met Mozart at this time and told him of the outstanding young musician in Bonn who needed to study with a leading composer-pianist to complete his musical education. At any rate, it was eventually arranged that Beethoven would visit Vienna to study with Mozart, and Maximilian Franz funded the trip. Beethoven probably took with him a letter of introduction from the elector; such letters were the usual way of making new contacts at the time. Despite Mozart's preoccupation with composition (in 1786 he completed *Le nozze di Figaro* (The Marriage of Figaro) and the following year *Don Giovanni*), it is significant that he was prepared to take Beethoven on, and he must quickly have been made aware that this was no ordinary pupil. Beethoven left Bonn in early 1787 and arrived in Vienna shortly afterwards. Unfortunately, he soon began receiving messages from home that his mother had become ill with consumption (tuberculosis) and might not live much longer. Thus he remained in Vienna for only a short time before returning home, receiving increasingly urgent letters from his father during the journey. It is uncertain how many lessons he had with Mozart, but he did at least make his acquaintance and may have heard him play (there are conflicting reports about this, and about how long he stayed in Vienna).

Beethoven's mother died on 17 July 1787, and two months later he recorded his deep sorrow in the first personal letter of his known to survive: 'She was to me such a good, lovable mother, my best friend. Oh!

---

[11] WR, p. 16.

who was happier than I, when I could still utter the sweet name of mother and it was heard and answered; and to whom can I say it now?'[12] As well as suffering deep emotional distress, he was affected mentally, physically, and from a practical point of view. His letter records that after her death he was suffering from depression ('Melankolie') and asthma, and was rarely happy. He also had to start taking responsibility for his family. His father began descending towards alcoholism and was sacked by the elector two years later, with half his salary thenceforth to be paid to Beethoven (though in the end it continued to be paid to the father to avoid embarrassment, and Johann passed it on to Beethoven). There were no aunts, uncles, or cousins in the vicinity, and all Beethoven's grandparents were dead. So too was his second cousin Franz Rovantini, a violinist who had lived with the Beethovens for a time until his sudden death in 1781 at the age of only 24. The family employed a housekeeper, but were unable to prevent the death of Beethoven's baby sister Maria Margaretha in November 1787. This left a family of just the father and three brothers, Ludwig, Carl, and Johann, and Ludwig as the eldest had to take charge whenever his father was unavailable or incapacitated. For other practical and emotional support they had to rely on friends such as the Breunings. Particularly helpful among the friends at this difficult time was the court violinist Franz Ries. Beethoven never forgot his kindness, and did much to help Ries's young son Ferdinand when the latter arrived in Vienna some years later.

All this domestic upheaval seems to have impacted on Beethoven's composing, for very little is known to have been written by him in the period 1787–9: there are the beginnings of a symphony in C minor; a fragment of a piano concerto that eventually emerged as No. 2 in B flat; and perhaps a few short piano pieces whose date is uncertain (a Bachian prelude in F minor, WoO 55, and two preludes in C, Op. 39, that pass through all the major keys in another obvious tribute to Bach's influence). This is very little compared with his output in earlier or later years, and it is possible that Beethoven was simply too busy. On the other hand far more survives from 1790–2, when there is no reason to suppose he was any less busy, and so it has been argued that he experienced a 'moratorium' on composition in the late 1780s for psychological reasons, akin to writer's block, in which his compositional activity lay dormant for a time,[13] before it burst out with renewed vigour in 1790. Beethoven once mentioned that he had experienced several such creatively dormant periods during his life; one of them may well have occurred at this time. Another possibility is that plenty was composed but was later lost, having in some cases perhaps progressed only to a less than finished state before being discarded. The

---

[12] A-1; BB-3.
[13] See Maynard Solomon, *Beethoven* (New York: Schirmer, 1977), pp. 29–30.

fragment of piano concerto provides tantalizing evidence that a large-scale work was being written, for it is a discarded page of full score from the middle of the first movement, and much more of this work must once have existed. If one such major work could be almost completely lost like this, there could well have been others.

The late Bonn works

Another reason for believing there to have been some lost works comes from Beethoven's next surviving substantial work. This is a cantata written to commemorate the death of Emperor Joseph II of Austria. Since he was the brother of the Elector of Cologne, his death on 20 February 1790 was felt particularly strongly in Bonn, where the first full opera season since the reopening of the opera theatre in early 1789 was promptly abandoned mid-season. The fact that Beethoven, rather than Neefe or someone else, was chosen to write the commemorative cantata is an indication that he was already highly regarded as a composer, and had therefore presumably been active in this field in the preceding years. The assuredness, variety, and originality of his writing in the cantata point in the same direction. He set to work with great alacrity, producing nearly 800 bars of music, and a performance of the *Trauerkantate auf Joseph des Zweiten Tod* (Funeral Cantata on the Death of Joseph II) was scheduled for 19 March, though it had to be cancelled for 'various reasons'. It may simply have been too long and difficult, or not ready in time. Wegeler mentions a cantata that Beethoven wrote in Bonn in which 'several sections were so difficult for the wind instruments that some musicians declared they could not possibly play them. As a result the performance was cancelled'.[14] Another friend, Nikolaus Simrock (a horn player and later a music publisher), had a similar recollection about a cantata: 'We had all manner of protests over the difficult places before us, and he asserted that each player must be able to perform his part correctly; we proved we couldn't, simply because all the figures were completely unusual, therein lay the difficulty.'[15] Both Wegeler and Simrock place this event in Mergentheim, which they and Beethoven visited in September 1791, but Wegeler states that the difficult cantata had been written somewhat earlier, and so it could well have been the *Joseph* cantata of 1790. Equally it could have been a cantata in honour of the new emperor, Leopold II, which Beethoven wrote soon after the *Joseph* cantata. Both cantatas seem not to have been performed at the time, and both were very difficult by the standards of the day, with many passages containing awkward or unusual figuration. Here then was a composer still only 19 years old, writing music that was too original and challenging for his peers and yet was thoroughly sound in construction

---

[14] WR, p. 22.
[15] TF, p. 106.

and technique. The autograph scores of both cantatas have long since disappeared, but a manuscript copy of them surfaced in 1884, and Brahms's initial reaction on seeing the score of the *Joseph* cantata is revealing:

> Even if there were no name on the title page none other could be conjectured – it is Beethoven through and through! The beautiful and noble pathos, sublime in its feeling and imagination, the intensity, perhaps violent in its expression, moreover the voice leading and declamation, and in the two outside sections all the characteristics which we may observe and associate with his later works.[16]

Beethoven's style was already distinctive and recognizable at this early age, and the effort he must have put into the cantatas suggests that he was both politically aware and thoroughly sympathetic to Joseph's liberal reforms.

One of these two cantatas was subsequently shown to Haydn. Haydn had been in the service of Prince Nikolaus Esterházy for many years, but the prince died in September 1790 and his successor Prince Anton, who had far less interest in music, promptly allowed Haydn to travel around Europe. Although many of his works best known today had not yet been written, his great reputation meant that there was no shortage of offers, and he duly set off for London, passing through Bonn on the way there (December 1790) and again on the way back (July 1792). On one or probably both of these occasions he met Beethoven, who showed him at least one of the cantatas. Haydn 'examined it very closely and then warmly encouraged the composer to continue his studies'.[17] It must have been at one of these meetings that the two men, along with Maximilian Franz, decided that Beethoven should travel to Vienna to study with Haydn and perfect his compositional technique, after the failed attempt to study with Mozart in 1787. As with the Mozart trip, it says much for Beethoven's extraordinary ability that Haydn was prepared to take on this new pupil, and that the elector was prepared to pay for him, after Beethoven had brought back 'nothing but debts' from his study with Mozart.

Before Beethoven finally set off to study with Haydn, however, he had continued to develop as a composer and pianist, supported not only by Maximilian Franz but also by Count Ferdinand Waldstein, who had arrived in Bonn in 1788 and did much in the ensuing years to support Beethoven unobtrusively. He was a composer and pianist himself, and

---

[16] Quoted from TF, p. 120.
[17] WR, p. 22.

Wegeler describes him as 'Beethoven's first and in every respect most important patron, his Maecenas'. Wegeler adds, 'It was he who in every way possible supported our Beethoven and first appreciated his genius to the full ... From him he often received financial support, bestowed with such consideration for his easily wounded feelings that Beethoven usually assumed they were small gratuities from the elector.'[18] In March 1791 Waldstein produced a ballet entitled *Ritterballett* (Knight's Ballet) for which Beethoven wrote the music, although it was given out that Waldstein himself was the composer, for reasons that are unclear. The music is delightfully light, energetic, and dance-like, and shows that Beethoven could readily vary his style to suit the occasion.

It was about this time that Beethoven also composed a violin concerto in C, or at least part of one. The first 259 bars, well over half the movement if it were of normal structure, survive in a manuscript in Vienna, and since the music breaks off at the end of a page it seems probable that the rest of the movement was completed. There is no sign of the finale, but the slow movement may have been an early version of Beethoven's Violin Romance in F, Op. 50. The autograph score of this, though written out in 1798, gives every impression that it is the middle movement of a larger work, since it has no proper title page or conclusion sign. It seems likely, therefore, that Beethoven revised the middle movement of his violin concerto in C at that time and then published it as a separate work.[19]

Neither the concerto fragment nor the ballet was published until the late nineteenth century, but one Beethoven work was published in 1791. This was a set of twenty-four variations on the theme 'Venni amore' by Vincenzo Righini. This work has had something of a strange subsequent history. It was reissued by a different publisher in 1802, and before long no copies of the original edition were known any more. Thus some writers suspected that the work must have been substantially revised for this reprint, since it was in such an advanced and sophisticated style. When a copy of the original edition was finally found in the 1980s, however, there proved to be no significant differences in the later version. Nothing better demonstrates Beethoven's extraordinary ability as a 20-year-old composer than this mistaken conclusion that the work as it stands belonged to the early 1800s. The Righini Variations form a truly remarkable work which in some ways even anticipates Beethoven's late style, for instance in the profound, timeless quality of the penultimate variation.

This same piece also demonstrates Beethoven's incredible ability as a pianist and as an improviser. In September 1791 Maximilian Franz travelled with his entourage and the court orchestra to Mergentheim, as mentioned

---

[18] WR, pp. 19–20.
[19] See Barry Cooper. 'Beethoven and the Double Bar', *Music & Letters*, 88 (2007), pp. 458–83, especially p. 469.

earlier. This involved sailing in two yachts up the Rhine and Main, and after passing through Mainz and Frankfurt they stopped at Aschaffenburg. Here Beethoven met the celebrated pianist and composer Johann Sterkel, as described by both Wegeler and Simrock.[20] The delicate and decorative style of Sterkel's playing was a revelation to Beethoven, whose own normal style was 'rough and hard' by comparison. When it came to Beethoven's turn at the keyboard, Sterkel suggested that the Righini Variations were too difficult for him actually to play. Beethoven then not only performed them (from memory), but adopted Sterkel's playing style exactly, playing 'as if these difficult variations were really as easy as a Sterkel sonata'. And, for good measure, he even improvised some additional and equally difficult variations! It is no wonder that the occasion stuck so firmly in the memories of Wegeler and Simrock that they independently produced very similar accounts some forty years later.

Beethoven's skill at extemporization became widely recognized from about this time. After reaching Mergentheim he met another pianist-composer, Carl Junker, who published a report of the meeting later that year. After praising the exceptional standard of the elector's orchestra, his report continues:

> I heard also one of the greatest pianists – the dear, good Bethofen ... I heard him extemporize; yes, I was even invited to propose to him a theme for variations. The great virtuosity of this dear, gentle-mannered man can in my opinion be safely estimated from the almost inexhaustible wealth of his ideas, the altogether distinctive style of expression in his playing, and the great skill with which he plays. Thus I know nothing that he still lacks in the greatness of an artist ... Even all the excellent members of this orchestra are his admirers, and all ears when he plays. Yet he is modesty itself, free from all pretension.[21]

With the publication of this report, Beethoven's reputation as a pianist and extemporizer spread far and wide, and the implication was that he was the best pianist Junker had heard, since Junker compared him favourably with another noted pianist, Abbé Georg Vogler. Beethoven himself, too, was no doubt aware that his playing was unsurpassed; but the modesty that Junker mentions is illustrated by Beethoven's restrained comment that he merely seldom found in other pianists the excellence that he felt he could justifiably expect.

Beethoven composed much else during his final few months in Bonn, and Haydn was probably shown more works than just one cantata when

---

[20] WR, p. 23; TF, p. 103. Simrock's account is in TDR, vol. 1, p. 266.
[21] TF, p. 105 (translation amended); TDR, vol. 1, p. 272.

they met in Bad Godesberg, just outside Bonn, in July 1792 during Haydn's return trip from London. Shortly after that, Beethoven began making preparations to travel to Vienna to study with Haydn, but events were hastened by external matters. War with France had broken out, and the French captured Mainz in October, thus threatening Bonn. Maximilian Franz temporarily left his residence on 22 October, and this no doubt seemed an opportune moment for Beethoven to fulfil his long-delayed plans to complete his studies in Vienna. Two days after the elector had left, Beethoven's friends began writing farewell messages for him in a small album. By the time he left, probably on 2 November, there were fourteen contributions,[22] some very short, others quite long. Two of them, by Count Waldstein and Johann Heinrich Crevelt, refer to Mozart's genius as a potential inspiration for Beethoven. Mozart had died the previous December but his music and his reputation lived on. The most famous entry in the album is Count Waldstein's:

> Dear Beethoven! You are now travelling to Vienna in fulfilment of your so long frustrated wishes. Mozart's genius still mourns and laments the death of its pupil. In the inexhaustible Haydn it found refuge but no occupation; through him it wishes once again to be united with someone. Through uninterrupted diligence may you receive: Mozart's spirit from Haydn's hands.

Waldstein probably sensed that Vienna needed a successor to Mozart, and Mozart was at this time the composer whom Beethoven most admired. Thus it was appropriate to suggest that Beethoven should inherit Mozart's spirit, even though Beethoven possessed a very different and distinctive personality, both in his music and in his life. Mozart's desire for an opulent lifestyle contrasts markedly with Beethoven's cautious, frugal nature. Mozart's love of billiards shows no echoes in Beethoven, who seems to have had no interest in games or frivolity. Yet both were outstanding in their improvisations, and there are countless passages in Beethoven's music, from both before and after he left Bonn, that contain something of Mozart's spirit and inspiration. Whether much of this was passed on by Haydn during Beethoven's lessons with him is doubtful, and to that extent Waldstein's remark may have been wide of the mark. But Beethoven certainly continued to display 'uninterrupted diligence' once he arrived in Vienna. Through this diligence and through hearing Mozart's music and even sometimes copying it out, Beethoven was able to absorb and appropriate Mozartian elements and blend them into his own musical style, thus effectively fulfilling what Waldstein had envisaged.

---

[22] All in TDR, vol. 1, pp. 496–502; translated in Alb-13.

Beethoven's sketches and autograph scores

Beethoven's extraordinary composing methods

Any good biography of a composer from the Classical period must be based largely on written documents of the time. Among such documents, those actually written by the subject are bound to be particularly revealing, and this is certainly true for Beethoven. He wrote numerous letters, memoranda, and other jottings, all of which can contribute to our overall understanding of his life, but four prose documents written by him stand out as being of exceptional interest: the so-called Heiligenstadt Testament of 1802; a letter to a woman known as the Immortal Beloved, written in 1812; a Tagebuch or memorandum book of personal thoughts, written piecemeal between 1812 and 1818; and a memorandum prepared for the Appeal Court in 1820. These documents alone would indicate a life well out of the ordinary, and they are so diverse in subject matter that between them they shed light on most of the main aspects of Beethoven's life. Each one has therefore been used as the basis of a separate section in the present book. The one thing they say very little about, however, is his music, and for documents concerning this it is best to turn to what are perhaps the most important ones of all, his music manuscripts, which are to be discussed at this point. They consist largely of sketches and autograph scores, along with a few other manuscripts such as correction lists that he sent to publishers, and copyists' scores that he amended. Most of his biographers seldom mention them, but they are of inestimable importance. If a composer such as Beethoven is interesting mainly because of the music he wrote, and his most frequent activity for most of his life was writing music, then logically much of our attention should be devoted to how he set about doing this; and the main type of source for such investigation is the music manuscripts. Here we can observe his masterpieces actually coming into being and taking shape. The manuscripts also provide vital clues that greatly illuminate his biography, especially in terms of chronology. Moreover, Beethoven's manuscripts are absolutely extraordinary in their appearance, quite apart from the undisputed quality of the music, and nothing like them is known elsewhere from his period.

When Beethoven left Bonn for Vienna in 1792, he took with him a large bundle of manuscripts that he had written, and he preserved them carefully for the rest of his life. As a result, there are over 400 leaves from his Bonn period still surviving today (including contemporary copies of his music written out by others).[1] They contain a mixture of sketches, autograph scores, and musical ideas that were never taken up in any known work. Some of these unused ideas appear to have been piano exercises to improve technique, written at a time when no published collections of keyboard studies were available. In some of the autograph scores empty spaces were later used for sketches, but 21 known leaves from Bonn are devoted exclusively to sketches and unused material.[2] It can be concluded, therefore, that even at this early stage Beethoven preferred to make some preliminary preparations before writing out a final version. This was not unusual for composers of the period, but already Beethoven was doing so to a greater extent than normal. His sketches usually show just the melodic outline of the music rather than the complete texture, and often the pitches of individual notes are ambiguous; he could presumably remember what notes he intended, including the harmony, and the sketch served mainly just as a reminder of the whole sound. Occasionally, however, he sketched the harmony instead of, or as well as, the melody. Often several works are jumbled together on a single page, making identification more difficult.

During the 1790s Beethoven gradually expanded the amount of sketching he did for new compositions, and many sketch leaves date from this period. Most of the autograph scores of works written during his early years in Vienna, however, are lost. Many of these were probably used by publishers when the works were being printed, and may well have been destroyed thereafter as possessing no further purpose. Beethoven continued, however, to hoard most of his sketches, which contained further fragments of piano exercises and random musical jottings (see Plate 3). He probably hoped to be able to make use of some ideas not yet adopted, and also he did not have time to sort out which pages could be discarded.

By 1798 his sketch leaves were becoming so numerous and jumbled that he decided to begin using proper manuscript books exclusively for writing new sketches. This was about the time

---

[1] Douglas Johnson, *Beethoven's Early Sketches in the 'Fischhof' Miscellany: Berlin: Autograph 28*, 2 vols (Ann Arbor, MI: UMI, 1980), vol. 1, p. 219.
[2] Ibid.

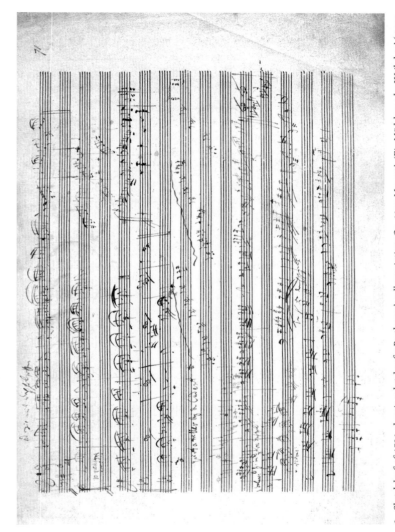

3. Sketch leaf of 1796, showing sketches for Beethoven's cello variations Op. 66 on Mozart's 'Ein Mädchen oder Weibchen' (staves 11–16) and some unused ideas or exercises.

when he embarked on his first set of string quartets, and the new sketching medium may have been a means of helping him to create more sophisticated music. He continued using such sketchbooks for the rest of his life, and over thirty full-sized ones still survive, although nearly all have had individual pages removed at some stage. Only through detailed study of such features as watermarks, ink blots, and stitch holes have scholars been able to work out where pages have been removed, and sometimes to locate the missing pages elsewhere.[3] Some of the sketchbooks were assembled professionally, but in many cases Beethoven himself put together a pile of loose leaves to form a home-made sketchbook, typically including more than one type of paper. Each book generally lasted him between six and twelve months. Such a systematic use of sketchbooks by a composer was quite unprecedented, and is one reason why he was able to compose music of such complexity and profundity. The pages of each book were used more or less in order (though not invariably so), and this often enables them to function as a kind of calendar of his composing activity. Works that can be dated by other means are often interspersed with undated works, enabling scholars to establish their approximate period of composition, sometimes to the nearest month or less. Beethoven continued to use loose leaves rather than sketchbooks from time to time – often between one sketchbook and the next – and there were some periods when all his known sketching was made on loose leaves, for instance in 1806. It is not always clear whether a whole sketchbook has gone missing or whether he went without one for several months.

Most of Beethoven's sketching during the early 1800s was written in ink, presumably at his desk or a table situated near his piano. Increasingly, however, pencil annotations and additions can be found in later sketches, and before long he was taking sheets of manuscript paper out with him on his customary long walks around Vienna or the nearby countryside, jotting down in pencil any good musical idea that came to him. He then established the habit of putting a substantial number of leaves together and folding them in half so that they fitted into his pocket. In this way he created a series of pocket sketchbooks. The earliest known is a very small one from 1811, but the rest are slightly larger and date from 1815 onwards. Nearly forty of these

---

[3] See especially Douglas Johnson (ed.), *The Beethoven Sketchbooks* (Oxford: Clarendon Press, 1985), where a complete chronological list of all Beethoven's known sketchbooks was first published.

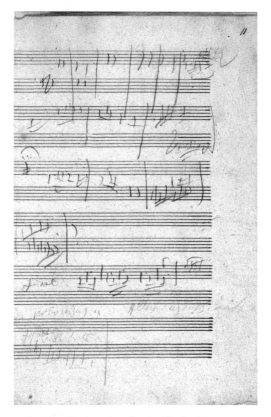

4. *Page from Beethoven's pocket sketchbook of summer 1825,*
showing Beethoven struggling to create the theme of the
'Cavatina' in the Quartet in B flat, Op. 130, and on stave 9
an idea for a possible theme for the finale of the quartet.

pocket sketchbooks are known, although the distinction between
a small number of leaves folded together and a proper pocket
sketchbook is not always clear-cut. This series did not supplant
the series of desk sketchbooks but ran concurrently with it: an
individual work would be sketched alternately in one or other
type of book, and both types must be studied to trace its progress
effectively.

During his final three years, which were devoted almost
exclusively to string quartets, Beethoven employed yet another
sketch format: loose bifolios (two leaves joined together) on
which the quartets were sketched in full score. This enabled him
to pay much more attention to details of part-writing than in
previous sketching (see Plate 5), and it is no coincidence that the
late quartets are very much more complex in this respect than

5. *Score sketch for a string quintet in C (WoO 62), which Beethoven was working on shortly before his death. The number of instruments filled in varies from bar to bar, as can be seen.*

any earlier ones, whether by him or by any other composer. Once again, the new sketch format did not supplant the previous two but was concurrent with both desk sketchbooks and pocket sketchbooks (and occasional loose-leaf sketches), making it even more difficult to trace the evolution of individual works.

At his death, therefore, Beethoven left a huge quantity of sketches, and around 10,000 pages of them are known today. Many more are lost: there are virtually no sketches for the First Symphony, for example, and it is inconceivable that he would have composed such a major work without extensive sketching. The surviving sketches were auctioned on 5 November 1827, a few months after his death, and were promptly dispersed. Most of the pages that survive are preserved in libraries in Berlin, Kraków, Vienna, Bonn, Paris, and London, and the rest are scattered in various libraries across Europe and the United States, with a few still in private hands. Detailed study of the sketches began in the second half of the nineteenth century, chiefly through the work of Gustav Nottebohm, and much further study has taken place since about 1960, although there is still a vast amount of investigation to be done. From such studies a picture has gradually been built up of the idiosyncratic way in which Beethoven composed.

The content and layout of the sketches themselves can be classified into several different types.[4] Some are brief ideas for possible new works; and since they were completely new ideas, Beethoven usually provided them with clefs, key signature, time signature, sometimes the harmony, and sometimes even a title (such as Sonata), to help him remember the precise character of the music. Such sketches are generally referred to as concept sketches, and often they remained undeveloped. On other occasions he gradually added other ideas, elaborations, developments, and possible continuations as he began intensive work on the new composition. These no longer needed key signature or time signature, which were by now firmly fixed in his head. He usually sketched a single-line melody, using or implying the treble clef, though other clefs can sometimes be found. Sometimes, when planning a movement or work, he wrote a synopsis sketch summarizing its main content – especially if the music was to have an unusual form or structure. These synopsis sketches are generally a mixture of notes and words, such as the names of keys or movements, or even parts of movements.

Once he had established the main features of the movement he attempted to fit them all together in a longer draft of perhaps fifty bars or more (see Plate 6), covering perhaps a whole exposition or even a complete movement. These drafts have come to be known as continuity drafts, since his main concern at this stage was to establish smooth continuity between different ideas, as well as the relative proportions of different sections within the draft. Often he wrote several successive drafts for the same passage, each one slightly more refined than the previous ones, though with occasional back-tracking to ideas that had been temporarily abandoned. In his early period he seems often to have been satisfied after making only one or two such drafts, but in later years he might easily write seven or eight continuity drafts for one section of music. In his late quartets, however, such drafts are rarely found in the actual sketchbooks, for he established continuity mainly in his score sketches.

Alongside the drafts he also jotted down numerous variant sketches as alternatives to individual phrases, and he worked particularly hard on the joins between sections, which is one reason why his music nearly always has such a strong sense of forward thrust and coherence between successive ideas. His mind was always so full of ideas, and he was so determined to find

---

[4] For a fuller account, see Barry Cooper, *Beethoven and the Creative Process* (Oxford: Clarendon Press, 1990), pp. 104–74.

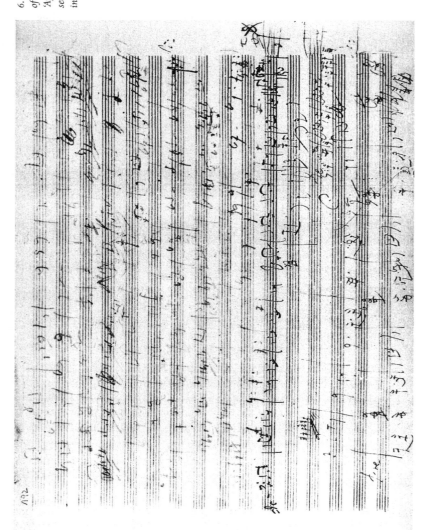

6. Page from Beethoven's sketchbook of 1804–5, showing sketches for the 'Appassionata' Sonata, with the distinctive second theme added on stave 11 in darker ink at a later stage.

the best one, that there are cases where he made over thirty sketches for a single phrase. The final draft in a sketchbook often corresponds almost exactly to the version in the autograph score, although of course it shows far less detail. Dynamics and articulation marks, indications of orchestration, and even harmony appear only infrequently among the sketches, while accidentals are often omitted too, especially where they are obviously intended.

Autograph scores

Writing the autograph score was, in Beethoven's mind, a different activity from sketching, and although his score sketches sometimes resemble fragments of autograph score they served a different function. The sketches were for private use only, and if nobody else could make sense of them (as was the case until Nottebohm's work) this did not matter to him. An autograph score, however, needed to be copied by someone for performance, and eventually published. Thus Beethoven had to try to make sure that all details were accurately in place, including all dynamics, articulation, ornament signs, and accidentals. He did not always succeed, but the intention was clearly there. He could then call upon any of several copyists, such as Wenzel Schlemmer and Wenzel Rampl, to prepare a neat version for performance or printing, although some works were printed directly from his autograph score. Occasionally he had to make a fair copy himself, if no copyist were available; this happened, for example, with his last quartet, Op. 135, which was completed at his brother's estate in Gneixendorf, a long way from the nearest reliable copyist. Normally, however, Beethoven wrote out just a single autograph score for each work. Although most autographs from his early period are lost, increasing numbers survive from works written after 1800, and autographs of nearly all of his works from the 1820s are known.

One might expect that, after so much preliminary sketching, Beethoven would have been able to write out a neat fair copy without any further difficulties, and some fairly neat autographs do survive. Good examples are the cadenzas that he wrote out around 1809 for his earlier piano concertos, for the benefit of his pupil Archduke Rudolph (see Plate 7). There is also an anecdote that his friend Marie Bigot, a highly gifted pianist, managed to sight-read the 'Appassionata' Sonata direct from Beethoven's autograph score when he called on her with the work on his way to the printers; and she did so despite 'many alterations and

7. Beginning of the cadenza for the first movement of Beethoven's Piano Concerto No. 1 in C; the cadenza was composed and written out neatly in 1809 for Archduke Rudolph.

erasures' in the manuscript.[5] Such alterations and erasures were extremely common in most of his autograph scores, especially the later ones. One reason was that he often began writing out the autograph score long before he had finished sketching the work, as is evident from a few incomplete scores for works that were abandoned, such as a symphony in C (1796), a piano concerto in D (1815), and a piano trio in F minor (1816). In each of these cases, the beginning of the score looks confident but it soon peters out, and the sketches show that Beethoven reached nowhere near the end of the first movement, let alone the end of the whole work. Many other works show enormous amounts of revision within the autograph score. Whole pages have sometimes been removed and replaced by a substitute, as can be seen by disruptions in the sequence of paper, as well as by the existence of discarded pages of score from some works. On other occasions so many amendments were made that the score became nearly illegible. A score for the first movement of the Cello Sonata Op. 69 is a particularly famous case, where the opening looks neat and confident but the development section is crammed with

---

[5] TF, p. 407.

8. *The final page of the autograph of the Kyrie in Beethoven's* Missa solemnis. *The revisions are so extensive that the last two bars of the string parts on staves 9–12 have been deleted and rewritten on the lowest four staves.*

deletions and amendments.[6] Another notable example is the Kyrie of the *Missa solemnis*, where the final pages in particular show massive revisions (see Plate 8). As with Beethoven's sketches, his repeated re-working of tiny details within the autograph score is in sharp contrast to the autographs of other composers. Bach's are a model of neatness by comparison, as are Mozart's; Handel's, though sometimes untidy and showing some changes, rarely come close to the kind of intensity of revision seen on page after page of many of Beethoven's scores. He clearly spent far more energy than other composers not only in his preliminary sketching but in his last-minute refinements, in an effort to create lasting works of art for the benefit of future generations as well as his own.

The significance of Beethoven's music manuscripts

Beethoven's music manuscripts are particularly important for enabling a far more detailed narrative of his life to be constructed than would be possible if one relied purely on other sources. A good example is provided by the three *Leonore* overtures, where the sketches greatly clarify the chronology. Although No. 1 is shorter and simpler than Nos 2 and 3, leading to speculation that it was composed first, the sketches show unequivocally that it was composed in 1807, after Nos 2 and 3.[7] With his ballet *Die Geschöpfe des Prometheus* (The Creatures of Prometheus, 1801), Beethoven's manuscripts not only illuminate chronology but also provide insights into the music itself. The main theme of the finale of the ballet also appears in a short dance piece, the contredanse WoO 14 No. 7, written about the same time. There has been much debate about whether the ballet incorporated a pre-existing contredanse or whether the contredanse was based on the finale of the ballet. Study of the autographs and sketches easily settles the issue: sketches for the ballet show the theme gradually taking shape, whereas the autograph score of the contredanse was not written out until at least six months after the premiere of the ballet.[8] Thus both sources confirm that the ballet was composed first. The theme itself was later used for a set of piano variations, Op. 35, before appearing in the finale of the *Eroica* Symphony. Recognizing that the *Eroica* is based partly on a

---

[6] See Lewis Lockwood, 'The Autograph of the First Movement of Beethoven's Sonata for Violoncello and Pianoforte, Opus 69', *The Music Forum*, 2 (1970), pp. 1–109.
[7] Alan Tyson, 'The Problem of Beethoven's "First" *Leonore* Overture', *Journal of the American Musicological Society*, 28 (1975), pp. 292–334. *Leonore* is the name generally used today for the early versions of Beethoven's opera *Fidelio*.
[8] See Cooper, *Beethoven*, pp. 111–12 (2nd edn, pp. 119–20).

heroic ballet, rather than a trifling contredanse, helps increase our understanding of what Beethoven was trying to achieve in the symphony. It is also fascinating to see, from the sketches, how he adopted the bass line from Op. 35 as the starting point for the creation of the opening theme of the whole symphony, a theme that was then modified to its present form but still shows an underlying connection to its origins. In fact his sketches often reveal intentional connections of this sort between different musical ideas – connections that would otherwise have remained speculative or even undetected.

Aside from biographical and musical insights, Beethoven's manuscripts are often of significance for establishing more accurate texts than are available in the early printed editions. These editions generally contain minor errors, and sometimes even quite major ones, that can be rectified only by consulting the autograph scores. For example, in the first movement of the Piano Sonata in E Op. 109, two whole bars were omitted in the first edition (bars 45 and 46), even though they had been in place when Beethoven corrected the proofs. The error crept in when the music was re-engraved before being published. Recent scholarly editors of Beethoven's music therefore always consult any autograph scores available, so as to obtain the best text.

Thus Beethoven's music manuscripts are of prime importance in many ways, and from a purely biographical point of view they tell us much more than any other source about the activity on which he spent by far the largest amount of time: composition. They reveal that his extraordinary works were the result of extraordinary compositional methods. Although the sketches may appear to show that he found composition very difficult, they actually show that he found it all too easy. He was full of so many ideas and possible alternatives that every work could have turned out in many different ways. It says much for his devotion to music, and his ambition to compose great works, that he spent so long sifting his ideas and selecting only the very best for the final version. Even then, although these versions may seem inevitable to us with hindsight, he could have continued refining and improving them almost *ad infinitum*. In a few cases a version that is later and arguably better than the one commonly known today still survives: this applies to both the Fourth Piano Concerto and the popular *Für Elise*.[9] For Beethoven, composition was not a

---

[9] See Barry Cooper, 'Beethoven's Revisions to his Fourth Piano Concerto', in Robin Stowell (ed.), *Performing Beethoven* (Cambridge: Cambridge University Press, 1994), pp. 23–48; Barry Cooper, 'Beethoven's Revisions to *Für Elise*', *The Musical Times*, 125 (1984), pp. 561–3.

matter of achieving perfection, but of aiming for the unattainable. As he himself wrote in 1812:

> The true artist has no pride; unfortunately he sees that art has no limits; he feels darkly how far he is from his goal, and while he is perhaps admired by others, he laments that he has not yet arrived at the place to where his better genius only shines a light for him like a distant sun.[10]

This desire for the sublime and the unattainable embodied the new spirit of the age at the dawn of Romanticism, and helped turn his works into models for the next generation of composers. As the rationalism of the eighteenth-century Enlightenment gave way to the ineffability of nineteenth-century Romanticism, Beethoven's highly individual attitude to composition became a yardstick by which the achievements of his successors could be measured throughout the rest of the century and beyond.

---

[10] A-376; BB-585.

TWO

THE CELEBRATED PIANIST
(1792–1802)

A student in Vienna

Beethoven's journey from Bonn to Vienna was not without incident. The French had already invaded the Rhineland, capturing Mainz in October 1792, and Beethoven therefore had to travel through a war zone to reach southern Germany and Austria. He kept a little memorandum book, known as his *Jugendtagebuch*, during the journey and for the next year or two, and this records that he gave the driver a tip 'because the fellow drove us at the risk of a cudgelling right through the Hessian army driving like

9. *The Kohlmarkt in Vienna, where the publishers Artaria & Co., who published many of Beethoven's works, had their premises (second to fourth arches from the right of the picture). There are several different versions of this drawing.*

the devil'.[1] Nevertheless he arrived safely in Vienna in November 1792, and promptly set about equipping himself with necessities that he had not brought with him. He first noted down 'wood, wig-maker, coffee', and then a longer list including 'overcoat, boots, shoes, piano desk, seal ... writing desk ... dancing-master'. He also copied down in his *Jugendtagebuch* an advertisement for pianos that was published on 10 November, which suggests he arrived in Vienna about that date. Later he confirmed, 'I have to equip myself completely anew.'[2]

Beethoven's shopping list tells us much about his daily life shortly after his arrival. His rooms were evidently heated by a wood stove, and he would need plenty of wood in winter, since Vienna has a continental climate that tends to be much colder in winter than the Atlantic climate of Bonn; he occasionally commented on the difference. He needed to buy a good overcoat and footwear, having presumably travelled with only the minimum of these. The piano desk and writing desk were essential for someone studying composition, and he always kept a desk beside his piano, so that he could quickly write down any interesting ideas that he happened to discover while extemporizing. Coffee was something of a luxury but was a drink that Beethoven enjoyed throughout his life in Vienna. The seal was a standard piece of equipment for sealing letters and documents at the time. A visit to a wig-maker was considered necessary, since wigs were still common, though they had all but disappeared within a few years; later portraits of Beethoven show him without a wig, unlike portraits of Haydn and Mozart. Dancing was an essential social accomplishment, and he noted down the name and address of a dancing-master, Andreas Lindner, whom he presumably visited. Ferdinand Ries, however, reports that Beethoven 'never learned to dance in time with the music' and was generally clumsy.[3] Ries's account of Beethoven's manner is clearly exaggerated ('He rarely picked up anything without dropping or breaking it'), but it makes the point that Beethoven lacked refinement of movement. Beethoven would surely have stood out in aristocratic Viennese circles, with his rough and unrestrained mannerisms, his strikingly regional accent, and his dark, swarthy complexion that gave him a Mediterranean appearance. Nevertheless, he was quickly welcomed by the aristocracy, particularly Prince Lichnowsky, in whose house he resided for two years or more. Since Count Waldstein was a distant relative of Lichnowsky, and Elector Maximilian Franz was related to the new Emperor Franz, the enthusiastic testimonials that they would surely have written enabled Beethoven to gain immediate acceptance by the

---

[1] Dagmar von Busch-Weise, 'Beethovens Jugendtagebuch', *Studien zur Musikwissenschaft*, 25 (1962), pp. 70–1.
[2] Ibid., pp. 72–3.
[3] WR, pp. 105–6.

10. *Miniature portrait of Beethoven, painted in 1802 by Christian Horneman (1765–1844). It is considered the best likeness of Beethoven from before 1812. In 1804 Beethoven sent the painting to Stephan von Breuning as a gesture of reconciliation after a quarrel, and it remained with the Breuning family for many years.*

11. *Prince Karl Lichnowsky (1761–1814). He was Beethoven's principal patron during the composer's early years in Vienna, and Beethoven even lived in his house for a time. In return the prince received dedications of several Beethoven works including his Trios Op. 1 and the* Pathétique *Sonata. Painted by an unknown artist.*

music-loving aristocracy of Vienna, who were no doubt duly impressed by his abilities as soon as they heard him at first hand.

Since Beethoven had come to Vienna for the specific purpose of studying composition with Haydn, it was not long before lessons were under way, and they continued for about fourteen months. Little is known about the course of these lessons, but there is no firm evidence to suggest, as sometimes claimed, that they did not go well or that the two composers did not get on together. Haydn helped Beethoven in numerous ways during the latter's first year in Vienna, lending him money when his allowance from Bonn did not arrive, and inviting him to Eisenstadt (where his patron Prince Esterházy resided) during the summer; Haydn went there in May and Beethoven followed on 19 June.[4] Other indications of the warmth of their friendship come from the *Jugendtagebuch*, where Beethoven records having paid 22 kreuzer for (drinking) chocolate for Haydn and himself, and on another occasion 6 kreuzer for coffee for them. As for the lessons themselves, Haydn generally preferred to teach composition by studying scores informally with his pupils, and probably did so with Beethoven too during most of the course of lessons. In addition, Beethoven wrote a batch of about 300 exercises in strict elementary counterpoint, of which 245 still survive. The uniformity of both ink and paper type, however, suggests that these exercises were not spread over a year but concentrated into quite a short span of time, perhaps as little as four to six weeks (his other music manuscripts from 1793 show a variety of ink and paper types). Haydn wrote corrections on some of the exercises, but left many mistakes uncorrected. Some writers have criticized him for adopting such a slack attitude; but this was not a correspondence course: Haydn and Beethoven were meeting regularly, perhaps three times a week, and there was no need to annotate all the errors, since they could be discussed verbally. What is more interesting is that Beethoven was making so many 'mistakes'. The rules of counterpoint were in some cases unnecessarily strict, and Beethoven was finding ideas that were satisfactory musically but in some way did not quite conform. He preferred to seek out rules for himself, which might not always coincide with traditional ones, and his tendency to strain the boundaries of acceptability formed an essential ingredient of his style throughout his life.

Haydn also oversaw Beethoven's latest efforts in composition during 1793, which included a set of variations for piano and violin (on 'Se vuol ballare' from Mozart's *Le nozze di Figaro*), an oboe concerto, a wind octet, and a wind quintet, plus a revision of the piano concerto in B flat that had probably been originally composed in Bonn a few years earlier. The oboe concerto is now lost, apart from its main themes and extensive sketches

---

[4] Alb-15; BB-8.

for the slow movement; the quintet also survives only incomplete. But the manuscript material that is known from these works is almost all on Viennese paper, confirming that all of them were written or at least completed after Beethoven had arrived there. Together the works are a major achievement, and Haydn was duly impressed. He sent a copy of the first four of them, plus an unidentified fugue, back to Maximilian Franz in November, along with a letter concluding that Beethoven would become 'one of the greatest musical artists in Europe, and I shall be proud to call myself his teacher'.[5] The elector's reply, that all these works except the fugue had already been heard in Bonn before Beethoven left, is clearly based on misinformation. It is of course possible that earlier versions had been heard in Bonn and that the works were merely revised in Vienna, but even this is unlikely, for if Beethoven were putting newly revised works in his package he would surely have included the B flat piano concerto. Thus suggestions in many biographies that Beethoven deceived Haydn, perhaps causing a rift between them, are mistaken.

According to Ries, Beethoven once claimed that he had 'never learned anything' from Haydn;[6] but this seems like another exaggeration, when one recalls Ries's claim that Beethoven 'never' learnt to dance in time and 'rarely' picked something up without dropping it. Beethoven clearly learnt an enormous amount from Haydn, even if the works he composed under Haydn's immediate tutelage show little or no direct benefit from the actual instruction. The course of lessons came to an end in January 1794, when Haydn left Vienna for his second and final visit to London.

This would have been an appropriate time for Beethoven to return to Bonn, but the political situation there was increasingly unstable, and by the end of the year the elector had been driven out by the French. Meanwhile Beethoven was allowed to remain in Vienna, though without any further salary from the elector. Beethoven's brother Carl moved to Vienna in 1794, and his other brother Johann joined them a year later, their father having died shortly after Beethoven's own move in 1792. Thus from 1795 onwards there was no family reason for any return to Bonn, and so Beethoven continued to reside in Vienna for the rest of his life, apart from short spells in the countryside most summers, usually in a village near Vienna; the most favoured villages were Baden, Mödling, Heiligenstadt, and Hetzendorf.

Instead of returning to Bonn, Beethoven continued his composition studies in a series of lessons with Johann Georg Albrechtsberger (1736–1809) that lasted over a year. Albrechtsberger had just become organist at St Stephen's Cathedral in Vienna and was thus effectively the foremost church musician in the land. He had also recently published a treatise on

---

[5] TF, p. 144.
[6] WR, p. 75.

composition (*Gründliche Anweisung zur Composition*, 1790) as well as one on figured bass, and was a renowned composer of counterpoint. His instruction of Beethoven was extraordinarily skilled and thorough, as can be seen from nearly 200 pages of exercises by Beethoven that still survive.[7] They consist mainly of exercises in specialized techniques (such as species counterpoint, fugue, and invertible counterpoint), gradually increasing in difficulty and complexity, and based on the old modes rather than the more modern system of keys. The fugues could be regarded as actual compositions, and they compare favourably with fugues written by many minor eighteenth-century composers. Albrechtsberger was nevertheless able to make quite a few improvements to these exercises, despite Beethoven's extensive previous training and his innate ability. Beethoven was kept so busy with this work that he composed very little other music during 1794, although he was beginning to prepare a set of piano trios and piano sonatas that would eventually emerge as his Opp. 1 and 2.

The rigorous tuition certainly left a mark on Beethoven's style, for his music tends to show more contrapuntal awareness of the movement of individual parts in 1795 than it had done in 1792–3.[8] The differences are not conspicuous, however, and imitative counterpoint remained fairly uncommon in Beethoven's music until his late period. Conversely there are examples of it even in the music he wrote in Bonn, since he had absorbed many of the principles of fugue-writing by learning Bach's *Das wohltemperirte Clavier* with Neefe. Thus it is difficult to identify individual passages in his works of the late 1790s that would have turned out differently without Albrechtsberger's instruction. The techniques learnt were nevertheless important in the long term.

Before the public as pianist and composer

Alongside his composition studies, Beethoven was working on his performing skills. He noted in his *Jugendtagebuch* that he was visiting Albrechtsberger and also 'Schupanzig', presumably the violinist Ignaz Schuppanzigh (1776–1830), three times a week each. Back in Bonn he had learnt the violin for some years, and he was evidently still playing the instrument. He also studied it in Vienna with Wenzel Krumpholz (c.1750–1817), according to Ries, who reports that in the early 1800s Beethoven used to play the violin part in his violin sonatas while Ries himself played the piano part.[9] Nevertheless, Beethoven's main instrument remained the piano, on which he no longer had anything to learn from any teacher. He worked at this by continuing to practise assiduously, inventing new

---

[7] 103 leaves are listed in Johnson, *Fischhof*, vol. 1, pp. 450–1; most have exercises on both sides. Many of the exercises are transcribed, with Albrechtsberger's revisions, in Gustav Nottebohm, *Beethoven's Studien* (Leipzig and Winterthur: Peters, 1873).

[8] See Lewis Lockwood, *Beethoven: The Music and the Life* (New York: Norton, 2003), pp. 83–4.

[9] WR, p. 106.

techniques and sonorities, which he sometimes jotted down among his sketches. No books of piano studies had been published at the time, and Beethoven invented his own exercises, working on such techniques as octave passages, double trills, and large leaps. He then made use of these when extemporizing before audiences, which he was doing quite often at this time. He claimed that rival pianists would sometimes adopt these ideas and pass them off as their own, and he actually published his *Figaro* Variations in order to prevent them from doing so.[10]

Beethoven's sketches indicate that he was also working on a revision of his B flat piano concerto around the end of 1794, followed by work on a new and strikingly original piano concerto, known as No. 1 in C major as it was his first concerto to be published. Having performed frequently at private music gatherings since his arrival in Vienna, he finally appeared in public on 29 March 1795 at a charity concert directed by the court composer Antonio Salieri (1750–1825) at the Burgtheater, in which Beethoven played a concerto. There has been much debate as to whether the work performed was his B flat or C major concerto; but the advertisement proclaimed that the concerto was 'entirely new', which suggests it must have been the C major work. Franz Wegeler, a friend from Bonn who had recently arrived in Vienna, reports that Beethoven finished his concerto only two days before the concert, and at the rehearsal the following day he found that the wind instruments were a semitone higher than his piano; he solved the problem by simply transposing his part that day to from C to C sharp. This provides a further indication that the C major concerto, not No. 2 in B flat, was played at the concert; No. 2 may have been played at a private event given by Prince Lobkowitz four weeks earlier, where Count Zinzendorf records that Beethoven made a deep impression but does not indicate what was played. On both of the two days after the public concert Beethoven was again in action, performing an extemporization on 30 March and a Mozart concerto the following day.

Having presented himself to the public as a leading pianist, Beethoven was keen to establish himself as a major composer, and invited subscriptions for what he called his Op. 1, a set of three trios for violin, cello, and piano, dedicated to Prince Lichnowsky and to be published by Artaria & Co. This was by no means his first publication or even his first Viennese publication (that was the *Figaro* Variations), but it was clearly intended to exhibit his best, latest, and most original work, and to announce to the world that he had arrived as a composer. Altogether 123 subscribers' names were collected by the time of publication in late August 1795, with 245 copies ordered. This was a very impressive total, albeit not nearly as large as Hummel's total of over 500 names for his Op. 3

---

[10] A-9; BB-11.

just two years earlier. The trios were probably first tried out at Prince Lichnowsky's, where Wegeler heard at least one of them before publication. Their formal introduction to the music world, however, took place a little later, shortly after Haydn's return from London in early September. Ries reports that Haydn attended the performance and made many complimentary remarks but advised Beethoven not to publish No. 3 in C minor. This report must be a distortion of events, either by Ries or by Beethoven (from whom Ries obtained the story), since the works were already in print by the time Haydn heard them. Haydn confirmed to Ries, however, that he had not expected No. 3 to be well received by the public, and had informed Beethoven of his view. As things turned out, the public generally agreed with Beethoven that No. 3 was the best of the three trios, with its powerful emotional content in a key that was to become very much associated with him.

These trios contained much that would have seemed extraordinary to the first listeners, who would have been struck not just by the dramatic power of No. 3 but by the rich textures, the vivacity and energy, and the intensity of the motivic development. Not surprisingly, the piano part demands a high level of technical ability, as does the violin part. More unexpectedly, Beethoven gave the cello part much more importance and interest than Haydn generally did in his trios for the same instruments, where his cello parts rarely do much more than play bass lines. Another striking feature of Beethoven's Op. 1 is his use of four movements, whereas Mozart's piano trios have only three and Haydn's either two or three. The message conveyed is that Beethoven was here working towards the four-movement symphony or string quartet, which were the pinnacles of instrumental writing and both of which normally had four movements by that date.

Beethoven's next significant publication was his Op. 2, a set of three piano sonatas dedicated appropriately to Haydn, who had done so much to help him during his early months in Vienna. These, too, are all in four movements and exhibit the same dynamism and originality as Op. 1, as well as pretensions to symphonic grandeur rather than the intimacy that was generally associated with the sonata at that date. Beside these major works, Beethoven was composing many shorter works in 1795 – arias, songs, variations, and ballroom dances – and his originality and technical command are repeatedly in evidence.

The trip to Berlin

While these works were being prepared for publication, along with Opp. 3 and 4 (a string trio and a string quintet), Beethoven set off around the beginning of February 1796 on a concert tour that was to take him northwards to Prague, Dresden, Leipzig, and Berlin. Lichnowsky travelled as far as Prague with him, and they stayed there for some time before

Beethoven travelled on to the other cities. These were the same ones that Mozart had visited with Lichnowsky in 1789, a fact that perhaps was seen to have symbolic significance, suggesting that Beethoven was Mozart's true heir. The days of the travelling virtuoso were still in their infancy, but Beethoven was able to make a great impression in the cities he visited. In Prague he wrote the recitative and aria *Ah! perfido*, and also some mandolin pieces, for Countess Josephine Clary, as well as several other works, and gave a few performances in February and March. His main destination, however, was probably Berlin and the court of King Friedrich Wilhelm II of Prussia. It seems that Beethoven planned to present a grand symphony while there, for sketches for such a work date back to 1795, and many further sketches were made during his concert tour. But he sensed that writing a work in the grandest of all instrumental genres would need much preparation, and he was not willing to produce a final version until he could be sure of its merits. Whether or not there would have been any opportunity for him to present such a work during his prolonged stay in Berlin is unclear, but he certainly did not make any effort to finish it hastily, and he brought his sketches back to Vienna for further development when he returned.

An important work that did result from his trip to Berlin, however, was his set of two cello sonatas Op. 5, which were probably commissioned by Friedrich Wilhelm. The king was a fine and enthusiastic cellist for whom Mozart had written some string quartets after his visit to Berlin in 1789, and had at his court two outstanding cellists in the Duport brothers, Jean-Pierre and Jean-Louis. The sonatas were probably written initially for Jean-Louis. The cello had been used increasingly as a solo instrument during the eighteenth century, accompanied by a bass line (often harpsichord or another cello) or sometimes even by a whole orchestra in a concerto. In other chamber music, however, it generally played a subordinate role. Even in violin sonatas the string instrument was usually subordinate to the piano, and only towards the end of the eighteenth century were the two instruments placed on a more equal footing. Cello sonatas of a similar type were much harder to compose, because of the problem of balancing a bass instrument against the piano. Beethoven was the first to tackle, and solve, this problem, and he used the cello in a great variety of ways, having already explored some of the possibilities in his Trios Op. 1. The size of the two cello sonatas is also impressive: although each consists of just two movements plus a slow introduction, the movements are symphonic in scale, with a sense of expansiveness that was virtually unprecedented in the sonata literature.

Beethoven wrote two other works for cello and piano while in Berlin – sets of variations on 'See the conqu'ring hero' (from Handel's *Judas Maccabaeus*) and 'Ein Mädchen oder Weibchen' (from Mozart's *Die Zauberflöte* (The Magic Flute)) – and most or all of his Quintet for Piano and Wind, Op. 16. He finally left the Prussian capital around early July 1796, having achieved great admiration from the king and his musicians, and having earned from the king as a reward a golden snuff-box full of coins.

Friendships in Vienna

Beethoven's return to Vienna was unmarked, but he was able to meet up with his brothers again and renew several old friendships, including that with his Bonn friend Lorenz von Breuning, who had been in Vienna since 1794. Lorenz remained until October 1797, when Beethoven wrote as a farewell message: 'Never shall I forget the time which I spent with you in Bonn as well as here. Hold fast your friendship for me, you will always find me the same.'[11] About this time Beethoven also wrote two pieces (WoO 51) for Lorenz's sister Eleonore. It has recently been discovered that these were written for a newly invented portable piano known as an orphica, and were independent pieces rather than the first two movements of a sonata in C for piano, as previously assumed.[12] It seems likely that Lorenz brought back an orphica for Eleonore from Vienna, the only place where such instruments were being made, when he returned to Bonn in 1797, along with Beethoven's two compositions for the instrument.

Another friend from Bonn, Eleonore's future husband Franz Wegeler, had already returned to his home city in 1796, but several other friends of Beethoven remained in Vienna. These included Prince Lichnowsky (who according to Lorenz von Breuning treated Beethoven just like a friend, despite their difference in class) and another nobleman, Baron Nikolaus Zmeskall (1759–1833), who was a fine cellist and often took part in Lichnowsky's concerts. Beethoven was in contact with Zmeskall for many years and often asked for his advice or assistance, but the friendship was never very deep: Beethoven regarded him as 'too weak for friendship'. Zmeskall and Schuppanzigh were mere 'instruments' on which Beethoven could play when he wished, and could never be true participants in his inner life.[13] A much more intimate friend was Krumpholz; he later introduced Beethoven to the budding pianist Carl Czerny, to whom Beethoven gave many lessons. When Krumpholz died suddenly on 2 May 1817, Beethoven was immediately moved to write a short choral piece (*Gesang der Mönche*, Song of the Monks, WoO 104) in his memory. Another man who became a very close friend of Beethoven, though only in Vienna for just over a year from spring 1798, was Karl Amenda, whose friendship Beethoven valued particularly highly. Beethoven regarded Amenda as one

---

[11] TF, p. 192.
[12] See Klaus Martin Kopitz, 'Beethoven as a Composer for the Orphica: A New Source for WoO 51', *The Beethoven Journal*, 22 (2007), pp. 25–30, and subsequent correspondence, ibid., 23 (2008), p. 47.
[13] A-53; BB-67.

of the three closest friends he had ever had, while Amenda expressed similar depth of feeling towards Beethoven.[14]

Two particularly important friends for Beethoven were Johann Andreas Streicher and his wife Nanette. They had moved from Augsburg to Vienna in 1794, and set up as piano manufacturers along with Nanette's brother Matthäus Andreas Stein. (The father of Nanette and Matthäus, Johann Andreas Stein, was also a noted piano maker.) This was an era in which many piano designs were being used, and modifications to the mechanism were frequently being introduced by manufacturers in attempts to make the instruments louder, more resonant, and more reliable. Viennese pianos had a much cleaner, purer, and lighter sound than English or French ones, although there were differences even between different Viennese models. Beethoven, as a leading pianist with an innovative, more singing style of playing that was more legato than most of his Viennese contemporaries, was able to have numerous discussions with the Streichers about possible improvements in design. He tended to favour their pianos above all others for many years, although he seems not to have been well acquainted with the technical and mechanical aspects of the instruments. He even set about promoting their pianos during a visit to Pressburg (Bratislava) and Pest (Budapest) in November 1796, performing on one of their instruments that had been specially sent out to Pressburg, at a concert on 23 November.

Making his mark as a composer

During the next two years or so, Beethoven continued composing energetically, establishing himself as the leading young composer in Vienna at a time when Haydn was approaching retirement. He had soon produced a series of masterly new chamber works that are still widely performed today, including piano sonatas (Opp. 7, 10, 13, and 14, and Op. 49 No. 1), violin sonatas (Op. 12), string trios (Opp. 8 and 9), a clarinet trio (Op. 11), and a variety of lesser works such as variations, songs, and a short sonata for piano duet (Op. 6). Little is known about his personal life during this period, however, and it has been suggested that he was seriously ill for some of this time, perhaps during summer 1797. One report mentions typhus, and it is possible that, if he did indeed contract this illness at this time, it could have initiated the hearing problems that ultimately resulted in near-total deafness some years later. The cause of his deafness, however, has never been satisfactorily resolved.

Of the works composed around this time, the most striking and still the most popular today is the *Sonate pathétique*, Op. 13. Exactly when it was

---

[14] The best summary of Beethoven's relationships with those around him, including Amenda, is provided in Peter Clive, *Beethoven and his World: A Biographical Dictionary* (Oxford: Oxford University Press, 2001).

composed is unclear since hardly any sketches survive, but it was published in December 1799, which suggests it was completed early that year, to allow for the customary six months' private ownership by whoever commissioned it, and was probably begun at least several months before that. It is a work of unprecedented power and intensity, in Beethoven's most characteristic key of C minor, and its emotional content, exploring the concept of pathos in musical terms, seems to herald the era of Romanticism, in which the sublime rather than the rational holds sway. From an analytical point of view, too, this sonata is highly original, with musical material from its slow introduction returning twice during the course of the first-movement Allegro, as well as appearing at one point in a speeded-up version as part of the Allegro. After a wonderfully rich Adagio movement, Beethoven dispenses with a minuet, which would have been difficult to reconcile with the mood of the sonata, and creates a finale that adapts motivic ideas from both of the first two movements, thereby producing an unusually unified work. Thus both emotionally and technically Beethoven was here pushing the bounds of Classical convention well beyond their previous limits, and the popularity of the work with experts and amateurs alike is well justified.

It was in summer 1798 that Beethoven embarked on his most ambitious project yet: a set of six string quartets commissioned by Prince Lobkowitz. Haydn and Mozart had brought the quartet to such a high degree of sophistication and perfection that, as mentioned earlier, Beethoven was cautious about composing a set of his own until he felt fully confident, and he even adopted a new method of sketching, using actual sketchbooks, to give him added support. Even then, it took him many months to produce the first three, which were not ready for Lobkowitz until October 1799, although Amenda had received a copy of No. 1 in F as a parting gift in June that year (this was the second quartet to be composed; Beethoven had begun with No. 3 in D). The remaining three quartets, Nos 4–6, were completed a year later, and were followed by substantial revisions to the first three. This cannot be proved for No. 3, but the copy of No. 1 that Amenda had received shows many significant differences from the standard published version. Beethoven wrote to him in 1801: 'Do not hand on your quartet to anybody, for I have greatly altered it, since only now do I know how to write quartets properly.'[15] No. 2 also underwent changes long after it was first completed, as can be seen from his sketchbooks. Thus Beethoven, like Mozart before him, had found the composition of a set of string quartets a difficult task, achievable only after a lengthy period of gestation during which other works were also written. Nevertheless the quartets, which were eventually published as Op. 18, do fully live up to the standards set by Haydn and Mozart, showing

---

[15] A-53; BB-67.

similar sophistication and skill in using each of the four instruments idiomatically, while varying the textures and blending the instruments together in original and imaginative ways. The quartets even surpass their models at times in terms of originality, notably with the slow introduction to the finale of No. 6, an evocative and deeply felt section entitled 'La malinconia' (Melancholy), which incorporates anguished chromaticism and tortuous modulations.

In May 1799 Beethoven received a surprise visit from Countess Anna von Brunsvik, who had come to Vienna from the Hungarian countryside to introduce her two eldest daughters Therese (1775–1861) and Josephine (1779–1821) to the social life of the city. Both daughters were capable pianists, and Beethoven gladly gave them lengthy piano lessons of several hours every day for the rest of their short stay in Vienna. Although he generally detested and avoided teaching, he was happy to make exceptions where the pupils were sufficiently talented, and his later pupils included Carl Czerny and Ferdinand Ries, both outstanding pianists. He quickly became a close friend of the Brunsvik family, visiting them at their Hungarian residences in Martonvásár and Budapest. Meanwhile Josephine hastily married Count Joseph Deym, who was nearly thirty years older than her, on 29 June 1799, and thereafter lived with him in Vienna until his death in 1804; but Therese remained single throughout her life.

During the two-year period of quartet composition Beethoven revised his two recent piano concertos. He wrote out a fresh autograph score of the B flat concerto in 1798, in time for a performance in Prague in October, but at this stage he did not actually write out the piano part, which he could play from memory with the option of extempore modifications. It was finally written down only in 1801, in a separate manuscript, when he was preparing the work for publication. The C major piano concerto was also performed in Prague in October 1798, before being revised and reaching its final form in 1800. In contrast to chamber works, concertos were often not published for several years but kept back so that each performance by the composer would be a noteworthy event, as well as providing an opportunity for revisions and improvements. Beethoven explained in 1801: 'Musical policy demands that one should keep one's best concertos to oneself for a time.'[16] Several of Mozart's piano concertos were not published until after his death, and Nos 1 and 2 by Beethoven were not brought out until they had been performed several times and gradually refined over several years. Unfortunately Beethoven's 'musical policy' has resulted in the partial loss of at least four works, for his other early concertos – the piano concerto in E flat, the triple concerto for flute, bassoon, and piano, the violin concerto in C, and the oboe concerto in F – were never published except as posthumous fragments or

---

[16] A-48; BB-59.

reconstructions. The piano concertos in B flat and C, however, did eventually reach printed form, as Opp. 19 and 15 respectively (since the C major was published first). Once these two works were published, no further revisions were made, although there are some intriguing alterations in the B flat concerto that were made just too late to be printed.

Beethoven also composed several new works at the very end of the eighteenth century. One was his Septet, which immediately became popular and remained so throughout his life, even after he himself had come to detest it. Another, even more significant, was his First Symphony, in C major. Having sketched three movements of a symphony in C during 1795–7, Beethoven seems to have run into difficulties over what to use for a finale, for he sketched several possible finale themes but did not find any of them suitable. Now, around the end of 1799, he decided to use his original first-movement theme for the finale and to build an entirely new symphony around this. No sketches survive for this new symphony, and so it was probably written very quickly, with the sketches confined mainly to a single sketchbook now lost. Hardly any sketches survive for the Septet either, and this was presumably sketched in the same sketchbook.

Some impressive performances

The symphony received its premiere at an *Akademie* presented and directed by Beethoven at the Burgtheater on Wednesday 2 April 1800, at 6.30 p.m. The programme was as follows:

Mozart, symphony
Haydn, soprano aria from *The Creation*
Beethoven, piano concerto
Beethoven, septet
Haydn, duet from *The Creation*
Beethoven, piano extemporization
Beethoven, 'new grand symphony' (No. 1)

Beethoven could have included one of his own orchestral arias, such as *Ah! perfido*, instead of Haydn's, but by including works by both Haydn and Mozart (though it is not clear precisely which ones) he seems to have been suggesting that he was their natural successor and that the three composers could be regarded as the embodiment of all that was best in music. Here then, for the first time, we find Haydn, Mozart, and Beethoven placed together as a triumvirate of great composers. The reviewer of the concert, though noting that the performance of the orchestra left much to be desired, especially in Beethoven's own compositions, which were difficult to play, asserted that this was 'truly the most interesting concert in a long time'.[17] If the Mozart symphony was his final one, the 'Jupiter',

---

[17] TF, p. 255.

12. *The Burgtheater, one of the two court theatres, scene of Beethoven's public debut in 1795, and also his first benefit concert in 1800; painted by an unknown artist.*

the audience would certainly have noticed some similarities between it and Beethoven's new symphony (for example, the shape of the theme in the opening Allegro movement, and the ingenuity of the handling of the themes); but they would also have noticed conspicuous differences, such as how Beethoven went far beyond Mozart in terms of energy and dynamism in the third-movement Menuetto, which is more of a scherzo than a traditional minuet.

Which piano concerto Beethoven played is also unconfirmed. He had been busy writing a new concerto in C minor in the preceding months. The sketches, like those for the symphony, are mostly lost; but the autograph score, though dated 1803, was written out mainly in 1800, as is evident from Beethoven's handwriting (particularly his system braces and double bars, both of which underwent substantial changes between 1800 and 1802). It therefore seems that he intended to perform this concerto at the 1800 concert, but it was clearly not ready in time, and so he probably substituted No. 1 in C major. This may even be the reason why he wrote out a fresh score of the work around that time.

Extemporization was common at the time, both in private meetings and at public concerts, and Beethoven had always excelled at the art. Thus it is no surprise that the reviewer reported that he extemporized 'in a masterly fashion' at the concert. Beethoven's skill in improvisation was again to the fore on another occasion shortly afterwards. About this time a celebrated travelling virtuoso named Daniel Steibelt came to Vienna, and there developed something of a rivalry between him and Beethoven, especially concerning their ability at extemporization. Matters came to a head when Steibelt performed an improvisation that had actually been prepared beforehand, using a theme by Joseph Weigl that Beethoven had used in the finale of his Clarinet Trio. Beethoven was irritated by this and, seizing the cello part of a Steibelt quintet that had been played earlier, placed it upside down on the piano, picked out a theme from the upside-down part, and improvised so magnificently that Steibelt left the room before the end, refusing ever to take part in an event alongside Beethoven again.

Beethoven also had a dispute with another travelling virtuoso, the horn player Johann Stich, after writing a horn sonata (Op. 17) for him about that time and performing it in Vienna and Budapest in April and May 1800. But he did not always fall out with other performers. Another pianist, Johann Baptist Cramer, had visited Vienna the previous winter (1799–1800) and the two men met frequently. Beethoven did not hold most pianists in high regard, but Cramer was an exception, and the only pianist whom he praised to Ries; Cramer had a high opinion of Beethoven too.

According to an anecdote told many years later by Cramer's widow, Beethoven and Cramer once heard a Mozart piano concerto being performed, and at one point near the end Beethoven was so delighted with the music that he said: 'Cramer, Cramer! we shall never be able to do anything like that.'[18] Cramer's widow identified the concerto as K. 491 in C minor, the most Beethovenian of Mozart's piano concertos; but she must have been mistaken (she was not present at the time), for this concerto was not published until several months after Cramer had left Vienna, and Mozart's widow Constanze, who owned his manuscripts, did not make them generally available, for fear that they might be copied illicitly. Moreover the concerto does not possess the musical features described by Mrs Cramer, and so she must have confused this concerto with another one (most likely K. 453). Nevertheless her anecdote is one of many indications of Beethoven's great admiration for Mozart.

Beethoven continued composing and performing privately during the remainder of 1800. He still had hopes of obtaining a permanent position of some sort, so that he could earn a regular income, but meanwhile he seems to have had no difficulty in selling his latest works to publishers; and that year Prince Lichnowsky generously granted him an annual stipend of 600 florins that was intended to keep him going until he secured an official post; the grant is a sign of Beethoven's extraordinary contributions as much as of the prince's generosity. Positions of music director, however, such as Haydn and Beethoven's grandfather had held, were scarce and becoming scarcer, as noblemen such as Prince Esterházy were devoting

---

18 TF, p. 209.

fewer resources to music than formerly and had mostly disbanded their regular orchestras. Positions at court were already occupied by composers such as Salieri, and were unlikely to become available. Thus Beethoven continued with his hand-to-mouth existence, and prepared for a hoped-for *Akademie* the following spring. Since he had a nearly-complete concerto ready (No. 3 in C minor), he began writing his Second Symphony. Work on this was interrupted during the winter, however, by a request from the ballet-master Salvatore Viganò for a ballet score, *Die Geschöpfe des Prometheus* (The Creatures of Prometheus, better translated nowadays as The Creations of Prometheus). This was a 'heroic-allegorical' ballet, in which the hero Prometheus creates two statues, male and female, brings them to life, and then civilizes them on Mount Parnassus through the power of the arts. The allegorical element was bound to appeal to Beethoven, with its image of the power of the artist uplifting humanity, and he set to work with great diligence, producing an impressive score that is rich in imaginative orchestration and strong rhythms suitable for dancing, but avoids his customary motivic complexity and long-range thrust, consisting of sixteen relatively short numbers preceded by an overture. The overture has since become popular, but the lovely music that follows is rarely heard. It is perhaps surprising that Viganò asked Beethoven, rather than one of the regular theatre composers in Vienna, to compose the music. Clearly Beethoven had made a wide impression by this time, and he was also eager to master every type of composition. His only previous ballet, *Ritterballett* (WoO 1), had been written in Bonn and was much shorter.

The premiere of *Prometheus* took place on 28 March 1801, and altogether the work received twenty-three performances in its first two years. This compares with only five performances of Beethoven's opera *Leonore* during its first two years (1805–6), and indicates that the ballet was a great success. Beethoven quickly prepared a piano arrangement of the entire score (an activity he normally left to others), and this version was published as early as June 1801. The finale was particularly popular, and Beethoven borrowed two themes from it when preparing a set of twelve orchestral contredanses (WoO 14) the following winter for use at society balls. He later used the main theme of the finale for two further works: a set of piano variations (Op. 35) and the *Eroica* Symphony. Self-borrowings of complete melodies or sections of music such as this are rare in his music, and were made only under exceptional circumstances: either the borrowed material had been discarded without publication; or it was used for minor ballroom dances (as with WoO 14) or for variations (Op. 35); or there was some extra-musical connection, as with the *Eroica* (Heroic) Symphony and the heroic *Prometheus* ballet.[19]

---

[19] See Cooper, *Beethoven and the Creative Process*, pp. 68–9.

Approaching deafness

All this time Beethoven was becoming increasingly troubled by his deafness and by the anxiety that, if it were discovered by others, his chances of success as a musician would be greatly diminished. Thus he made every effort to conceal it, except from a few doctors who tried unsuccessfully to treat it. Eventually at the end of June he confided in two trusted friends who were no longer living in Vienna – Wegeler and Amenda – and wrote long letters to both, dated 29 June and 1 July respectively.[20] To Wegeler he begins positively, outlining some of his successes: 'My compositions bring me much in, and I can say that I have almost more commissions than I can carry out. Also for every composition I have 6, 7 publishers and even more, if I want to make use of them; people no longer bargain with me, I demand and they pay.' His successes had indeed been quite remarkable. But then, turning to his difficulties, he writes a detailed account of his illnesses, aware that Wegeler as a doctor would understand and perhaps even be able to make recommendations. 'My hearing has become ever weaker for 3 years, and supposedly through my abdomen, which as you know was already wretched before, but has here become worse in that I have been constantly afflicted with diarrhoea, and consequently have been suffering with an extraordinary weakness.' He describes various remedies that doctors had prescribed: strengthening medicines, almond oil, cold baths, tepid baths, pills for his stomach, and an infusion for his ear. None of these had improved his hearing, though his abdomen had improved somewhat. After a detailed description of his hearing symptoms, which included tinnitus and inability to hear soft speech, he then reaches an emotional climax: 'Already I have often cursed my Creator and my existence. Plutarch has led me to resignation; I will if it is at all possible defy my fate, though there will be moments in my life when I shall be the most unfortunate of God's creatures ... Resignation, what a wretched resource! Yet it is all that is left to me.' He concludes with a variety of comments mainly about friends known to both him and Wegeler. The letter to Amenda, though less detailed, mentions all the main points: the successful sales of his compositions, the three years of problems with hearing, the cursing of his Creator, the improvements in his abdomen, the support he has had from Lichnowsky, and the recourse to 'sad resignation'. This could refer to resignation from public life and the life of a performing virtuoso, for in both letters he mentions that he is having to withdraw from society in general.

It is difficult to imagine the extreme suffering that Beethoven must have undergone at this time, with misplaced hopes of cure repeatedly dashed; fear that his perceived 'enemies' would take advantage; and anxiety that he would not achieve what he and others had come to expect from his

---

[20] A-51 and A-53; BB-65 and BB-67.

amazing talent. Yet through all this summer of 1801 he continued composing assiduously: four piano sonatas can be dated to this period, Opp. 26, 27 (two sonatas), and 28, and he was soon returning to his Second Symphony in preparation for the following spring. He found, in fact, that his deafness troubled him least when he was composing, since he could hear in his head all the sounds he wished to create, and also knew, like many good musicians, how to represent those sounds on paper, as surely as most people know how to represent on paper the sounds of vowels and consonants.

A second letter to Wegeler followed in November. Beethoven updates information on the treatments he had been receiving and laments that his hearing is no better, but he shows a more positive outlook. He states that the change is due to 'a dear charming girl who loves me and whom I love'; this is believed to have been Countess Julie (or Giulietta) Guicciardi, a cousin of the Brunsvik girls. He would, but for his deafness, have undertaken more concert tours across 'half the world'. However, instead of resorting to resignation that he cannot do this, he now expresses an intention to work ceaselessly, and to 'seize Fate by the throat; it shall certainly not crush me completely'.[21] This overwhelming desire to overcome all misfortune is central to Beethoven's character. He had enormous determination to cure his deafness if at all possible – hence his willingness to undergo treatments that were at best inconvenient and at worst painful and ineffective – but was adjusting to the possibility of having to live with his deafness permanently, composing rather than performing. His years as a celebrated pianist were coming to an end.

During the winter Beethoven visited the Guicciardi household from time to time, generously giving Julie piano lessons without payment. When he received a gift from her mother Susanna in January 1802, however, he was furious and very nearly sent it back, since it appeared to place him in her debt. He loved to give freely of his time and talents whenever he could, and this gift had undermined that desire. In a letter to Susanna he vowed, 'as revenge', to place the Guicciardis eternally in debt to him.[22] But how could this be accomplished? Two months later, in March, the wonderful 'Moonlight' Sonata was published with a dedication to Julie (the dedication was printed in Italian, with her name given as Giulietta). This was Beethoven's revenge, for the Guicciardi name was spread far and wide as the sonata quickly gained the extraordinary popularity it has enjoyed ever since. It was a gift that could never be either returned or adequately recompensed.

---

[21] A-54; BB-70. For confirmation that the girl's real name was Julie, not Giulietta, and other new information about her background, see Rita Steblin, '"A dear, enchanting girl who loves me and whom I love": New Facts about Beethoven's Beloved Pupil Julie Guicciardi', *Bonner Beethoven-Studien*, 8 (2009), pp. 89–152.

[22] Alb-36; BB-77.

13. *The village of Heiligenstadt, where Beethoven stayed for six months in 1802, during which time he wrote his Heiligenstadt Testament. He also stayed there in 1808 while composing the* Pastoral Symphony.

Beethoven planned to perform his Second Symphony and his C minor piano concerto at an *Akademie* in April, but he was unable to obtain a day for the concert and the expected slot was allocated to very inferior musicians, which made him angry once again. Shortly after this, in a final attempt to cure his deafness, he moved to the small village of Heiligenstadt, about three miles north of the centre of Vienna (and today a suburb), to spend six months in quiet surroundings away from the noise and dirt of the city. While there he claimed to be leading a rather lazy life, but actually he was quite busy writing three piano sonatas commissioned by the Zurich publisher Johann Georg Nägeli, as well as working on two extra-ordinary new sets of variations (Opp. 34 and 35), which were temporarily set aside to allow rapid completion of the three sonatas. When October finally arrived, however, and it was time to return to Vienna, Beethoven realized that his deafness was no better. He had reached a low point in his life. Misfortune in love and friendship with the Guicciardis (he had, as he claimed years later, rejected Julie, who then married Count Wenzel Gallenberg in 1803), added to professional disappointment over the concert he had been denied, was now compounded by the loss of his last hope of a cure for his deafness. In despair, he sat down to write what has become known as his Heiligenstadt Testament, which marked a turning point in his life. It is such an important and revealing document that it will be quoted in full in the section that follows.

Beethoven's deafness: the Heiligenstadt Testament

The Testament

In October 1802 Beethoven wrote out his famous Heiligenstadt Testament, as follows.[1]

> For my brothers Carl and [Johann van] Beethoven.
> O you people who think or say that I am hostile, stubborn, or misanthropic, how greatly you wrong me. You do not know the secret cause which makes me seem so to you. From childhood on, my heart and soul have been full of the tender feeling of goodwill, and I was always desirous to accomplish great deeds. But just think, for six years an incurable condition has befallen me, made worse by incompetent doctors, from year to year deceived with the hope of getting better, finally forced to the prospect of a <u>lasting infirmity</u> (whose cure will perhaps take years or even be impossible). Though born with a fiery, lively temperament, receptive to the diversions of society, I soon had to withdraw myself, to spend my life alone. And if I wished at times to ignore all this, oh how harshly was I then driven back through the doubly sad experience of my bad hearing; and yet it was not yet possible for me to say to people, 'Speak louder, shout, for I am deaf.' Oh how could I possibly admit weakness of the <u>one sense</u> which should be in me at a more perfect level than in others, a sense which I once possessed in the greatest perfection, a perfection such as few indeed in my profession have or ever have had?
> Oh I cannot do it; so forgive me if you should see me draw back when I would gladly have mingled with you. My misfortune is doubly painful to me as I am bound to be misunderstood because of it; for me there can be no relaxation in human company, no refined conversations or mutual outpourings. I must live like an outcast, quite alone, entering society practically only as much as real necessity demands. If I approach people a burning

---

[1] The translation is based on that in Barry Cooper (ed.), *The Beethoven Compendium* (London: Thames & Hudson, 1991), pp. 170–1.

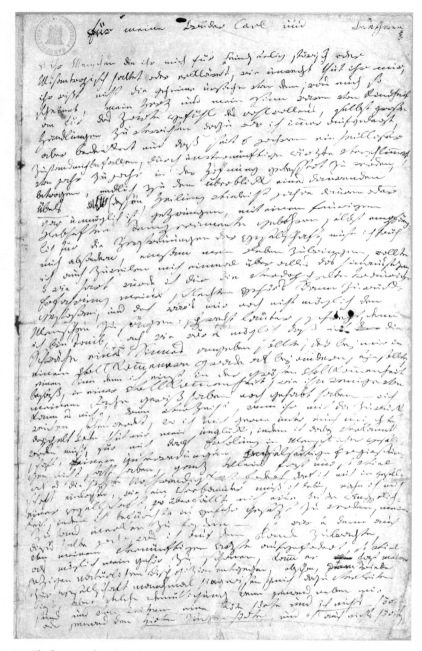

14. *The first page of Beethoven's Heiligenstadt Testament of October 1802, addressed to his brothers Carl and [Johann van] Beethoven.*

anxiety comes over me, in that I fear being placed in danger of my condition being noticed.

It has been like this also during the last six months, which I spent in the country. My sensible doctor, by ordering me to spare my hearing as much as possible, almost came to my own present natural disposition, although I sometimes let myself be seduced by my love of companionship. But what humiliation for me when someone standing near me heard a flute in the distance and I heard nothing, or someone heard the shepherd singing and again I heard nothing. Such incidents brought me near to despair; a little more and I would have ended my life.

Only art held me back. Ah, it seemed to me impossible to leave the world until I had produced all that I felt was within me; and so I spared this wretched life – truly wretched for so sensitive a body, where a rapid change can reduce me from the best condition to the worst.

Patience, they say, is what I must now choose for my guide, and I have done so. I hope my determination will firmly endure until it pleases the inexorable Parcae to break the thread. Perhaps I shall get better, perhaps not; I am prepared.

Already forced to become a philosopher in my 28th year, it is not easy, and for the artist harder than for anyone else.

Godhead, you look down on my inmost being and know it; you know that therein dwells the love of humanity and the inclination to do good. People, when at some point you read this, consider that you have done me an injustice; and the unfortunate may console themselves to find a similar case to theirs, who despite all the limitations of nature yet did everything he could to be admitted to the ranks of worthy artists and people.

You, my brothers Carl and [Johann], as soon as I am dead, if Professor Schmidt is still alive, ask him in my name to describe my disease, and attach this written document to his account of my illness, so that at least as much as possible the world will be reconciled to me after my death.

At the same time I here declare you both to be the heirs of my small fortune (if you can call it that); divide it fairly, and bear with and help each other. What you did against me you know was long ago forgiven. You, brother Carl, I thank in particular for your recent proven attachment to me. My wish is that you both have a better, more trouble-free life than I have had. Recommend <u>virtue</u> to your children; it alone, not money, can provide happiness. I speak from experience – that was what raised me in my wretchedness; thanks to it and to my art, I did not end my life by suicide.

Farewell and love each other. I thank all my friends, particularly <u>Prince Lichnowsky</u> and <u>Professor Schmidt</u>.

I want the instruments from Prince L. to be preserved by one of you, yet not to cause strife between you; but as soon as it is more useful to you, just sell them. How happy I am if I can still be of use to you in my grave – were it to happen – with joy I hasten towards death. If it comes before I have had the chance to develop all my artistic abilities, then despite my harsh fate it will still be coming too soon and I should probably wish it later. Yet even then I should be content, for would it not free me from a state of endless suffering? Come when you will, I shall approach you bravely.

Farewell, and do not completely forget me when I am dead. I have deserved this from you, in that during my life I often thought of how to make you happy; do be so.

Ludwig van Beethoven

Heiglnstadt
6 October 1802

For my brothers Carl and [Johann]
to be read and executed after my death.

Heiglnstadt, 10 October 1802, thus I take leave of you – and indeed sadly. Yes the fond hope which I brought here with me to be cured at least to a certain extent – it must now wholly abandon me. As the leaves of autumn fall and wither, so too has my hope dried up; I go away almost as I came. The high courage itself which often inspired me in the fine days of summer has vanished.

O Providence, grant me some time a pure day <u>of joy</u>. For so long now the heartfelt echo of true joy has been strange to me. Oh when – oh when, O Godhead – can I feel it again in the temple of nature and of humanity. Never? No – oh that would be too hard.

Rarely if ever has a composer written such a poignant document about his misfortune. Beethoven preserved the Heiligenstadt

Testament carefully throughout his life, and it was discovered among his papers shortly after his death, since when it has been the subject of much discussion.[2] Although its primary cause and topic was his increasing and persistent deafness, it covers a wide range of other matters, placed into a structure that, though owing something to the principles of classical rhetoric, wanders from the central issue at several points. Yet it is no series of random jottings, for the neatness of the script suggests much preliminary preparation, and several sketches comparable to those for his compositions may well have been made.

During the course of the text there are several changes in who is being addressed. The heading indicates the document is intended for Beethoven's brothers; and curiously he omitted the names of both Caspar Carl and Nikolaus Johann at first, for unknown reasons, before inserting Carl's name (but not Johann's) slightly later, as can be deduced from the spacing in the original document. Yet the first paragraph is not addressed specifically to them but to everyone who thought he was 'hostile, stubborn, or misanthropic'. Later in the Testament Beethoven addresses God directly, though calling him 'Gottheit' ('Godhead') rather than simply 'God'. Finally, having addressed the world in general and God himself, Beethoven turns to his brothers themselves, for whom he felt a certain responsibility as the head of the family ever since the deaths of their parents. Then, in a postscript added four days after he had begun the initial draft (which may have been completed over more than just a single day), he addresses the village of Heiligenstadt, the source of his hope and ultimately his despair, bidding it farewell before turning once again to God (now addressed as 'Vorsehung', Providence) in a plea for happier times.

Many of the statements in the Testament resonate with elements of Beethoven's life known from elsewhere. His direct pleas to God are typical of his approach to religion, while his reference to the Parcae, the Fates of classical antiquity, reflects his knowledge and love of ancient writers. His recourse to patience as a guide recalls his references to resignation in earlier letters to Wegeler and Amenda, and his desire for a day of pure joy ultimately found a kind of fulfilment in his setting of Schiller's *An die Freude* (To Joy) in his Ninth Symphony. His opening comment on the popular view of his character is quite perceptive, for even today he is easily perceived as someone who railed against the world and stubbornly refused to change a note of his compositions

---

[2] For a penetrating psychological interpretation, see Solomon, *Beethoven*, pp. 118–21.

when performers found them difficult. He was equally perspicacious when judging his own character, noting his 'fiery … temperament' and love of companionship, while his references to having always had a 'tender feeling of goodwill' and his recommendation of virtue above all else were in no way expressions of false piety: he genuinely was a thoroughly good, upright, and kind character, as confirmed by several observers such as Ignaz von Seyfried:

> Justice, personal decency, the moral code, a devout mind and religious purity meant more to him than all else; these virtues were enthroned in him and he demanded that others cultivate them … He took pleasure in helping others out of pure love for his neighbour, only too often making considerable sacrifices, greatly to his own disadvantage.[3]

The course of Beethoven's deafness

As mentioned earlier, the precise cause and nature of Beethoven's deafness have never been determined (see Chapter Six, 'Myths about Beethoven', for some of the suggested but implausible causes), although it appears to have been centred on the auditory nerves themselves. The initial onset has also not been precisely dated, for in the Testament Beethoven says he has been affected 'for six years', yet in his letter to Wegeler of June 1801 he stated that his hearing had been deteriorating for only three years. Thus a date of around late 1797 or early 1798 is the nearest that can be surmised from these conflicting statements. The early symptoms, as described in his letter to Wegeler, were of humming and buzzing in his ears (tinnitus), difficulty in deciphering speech, and inability to hear high notes from a distance – the latter problem illustrated by the reference in the Testament to a distant flute that he could not hear. (Ferdinand Ries reports a similar occasion when Beethoven could not hear a shepherd's flute that had attracted Ries's attention.)

In 1802 Beethoven still felt obliged to keep his deafness secret, and it is not clear how long he successfully kept this up. Czerny reports that when he first visited Beethoven at about the age of ten, probably in 1801, he already noticed that Beethoven had some cotton (or cotton-wool) in his ears, and it must have soon become common knowledge that Beethoven was having some

---

[3] Quoted from O. G. Sonneck, ed., *Beethoven: Impressions by his Contemporaries* (New York: Schirmer, 1926, repr. New York: Dover, 1967), p. 46.

kind of hearing difficulty. It was late 1806, however, before he felt confident enough to write (among the sketches for the third 'Razumovsky' Quartet): 'Let your deafness be no more a secret – even in art.' His hearing does not seem to have deteriorated significantly during the next few years, and he continued performing on the piano, notably at the public premiere of his Fourth Piano Concerto in 1808. But such events were far less frequent than during his first decade in Vienna. In 1811 he noted on the first page of the Petter Sketchbook: 'Cotton-wool in my ears at the piano frees my hearing from unpleasant buzzing.'[4] Thus he was still suffering from some form of tinnitus, although his hearing was not conspicuously worse. It seems to have begun deteriorating significantly again, a year or two later, however, and he asked Johann Maelzel (inventor of the metronome) to make some ear-trumpets for him. Maelzel duly obliged with a number of different designs, some of which were more effective than others, and Beethoven continued to use them for a number of years.

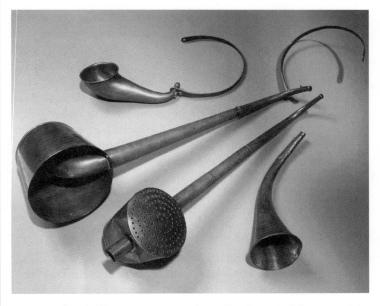

15. A selection of Beethoven's ear-trumpets, designed by Johann Maelzel, inventor of the metronome, during the period 1812–14 to assist Beethoven's poor hearing.

[4] Bonn, Beethoven-Archiv, Mh 59, f. 1r. See TF, p. 473, where the inscription is wrongly dated 1809. The subsequent development of Beethoven's deafness is conveniently summarized in George Thomas Ealy, 'Of Ear Trumpets and a Resonance Plate: Early Hearing Aids and Beethoven's Hearing Perception', *19th-Century Music*, 17 (1993–4), pp. 262–73.

By 1818, however, his hearing had deteriorated so much that he had difficulty with conversations even when using an ear-trumpet. Thus he took to using conversation books, in which his acquaintances wrote down their side of the conversation (see Chapter Five). His hearing sometimes underwent temporary improvements even then, and some of these may have meant that he could avoid using conversation books on certain days. Even as late as 1823 one writer, Johann Reinhold Schultz, visited Beethoven and reported that, if one spoke slowly and loudly, he would generally understand. Beethoven also frequently used a slate instead of a notebook, in which case each conversation was quickly erased. A slate was less convenient to carry around, however, and so a conversation book was usually used when he was dining at a restaurant.

Beethoven's deafness was not as comprehensive as is sometimes imagined. He did not start to go deaf until he was nearly 30; he could still hear tolerably well, and give performances on the piano, up to the age of 40, and he needed conversation books only for the last nine years of his life (1818–27), when he was profoundly deaf. Even at the very end of his life, however, he was never quite totally deaf, and his very last action was to react to a loud thunder-clap by raising an arm from his deathbed.

It is impossible to say how much his music was affected by his deafness. Had he not gone deaf he would probably have performed far more, and consequently composed far less; thus his loss is our gain. He would also probably have composed more piano concertos, since these were ideal vehicles for innovations in piano technique. His later music tends to become more cerebral and less improvisatory, and this may be a result of his declining tendency to try things out at the piano. But it is pure speculation to imagine what his later music might have sounded like if he had not gone deaf, and it would probably not have been very different, since he relied mainly on his inner ear rather than the sounds around him. It would also be rash to interpret any of his purely instrumental compositions as an explicit response to his deafness, since the sketches provide no evidence that they are. The one work that does appear to be a direct response is his oratorio *Christus am Oelberge* (Christ on the Mount of Olives). This was the first major work he composed after the Heiligenstadt Testament and, although it makes no reference to deafness, it focuses very strongly on the issue of extreme suffering and ultimate triumph over it. Some of the text has strikingly close parallels to parts of the Heiligenstadt Testament and letters that Beethoven had written to Wegeler and Amenda about his deafness in 1801.[5] Thus it seems highly probable that, having written the Testament and resolved not to commit suicide but to overcome his affliction, he searched for a subject that was emotionally in some ways parallel to his personal anguish, and found it in Christ's agony on the Mount of Olives. The libretto was then written within about a fortnight by a local poet, Franz Xaver Huber, whom Beethoven consulted frequently during the creation of the text, and it was quickly set to music. The Heiligenstadt Testament itself, however, is Beethoven's most significant and direct response to his deafness crisis, and it marked a turning point in his career. For many, in fact, it marks the start of his 'second period', in which his style moved much further from Classical norms as he embarked on a series of impressively large-scale, difficult, and complex works that are among his most popular today: the *Eroica*, Fifth, and *Pastoral* Symphonies, the Violin Concerto, the 'Waldstein' and 'Appassionata' Sonatas, the 'Razumovsky' Quartets, and *Fidelio*.

---

[5] See Barry Cooper, 'Beethoven's Oratorio and the Heiligenstadt Testament', *The Beethoven Journal*, 10 (1995), pp. 19–24.

THREE

THE HEROIC COMPOSER (1802–1808)

A new way

'I am not very well satisfied with the work I have done so far. From now on I intend to take a new way.' So said Beethoven, according to Czerny, shortly before the publication of the three piano sonatas (Op. 31) written for Nägeli.[1] The works Beethoven had in mind, however, were probably not these sonatas but the two sets of variations (Opp. 34 and 35) that he had begun in Heiligenstadt and completed shortly after his return, for he told his publisher Breitkopf & Härtel that, although he did not normally notice innovations in his own works, these two revealed an entirely new approach. In the first set, the theme is not varied and decorated in the traditional way but is transformed in character, with each successive variation being in a different key and metre, so that the gentle adagio theme in F might become a lively 6/8 gallop in B flat, a mournful funeral march in C minor, or an elegant minuet in E flat, while retaining its original melodic outline. The second set is equally extraordinary. It is based on the theme from the finale of Beethoven's *Prometheus* ballet, but the work starts out with a bare, unaccompanied bass line. This might not be so bizarre if the bass had a recognizable melody, like a Baroque chaconne, but this *Prometheus* bass line has no proper 'tune', with some bars occupied by either a single note, a complete rest, or a little fragment that scarcely sounds like a motif. Next there appear several variations on the bass line before the main theme is heard; and at the end, after a series of fifteen variations, there is a magnificent fugue based on the first four notes of the original bass line, followed by further variations. Beethoven was absolutely right in indicating that both sets of variations were utterly different from anything that had gone before, and he decided to give them proper opus numbers to highlight their importance (all his earlier sets of variations had had no opus number).

---

[1] TDR, vol. 2, p. 362.

These two works thus reveal Beethoven to be raising his sights, aiming for greater power, length, and complexity than in previous works of the same genre; the *Prometheus* set is particularly impressive in this respect. These elevated aims then became a hallmark of his middle period. On 23 November 1802 his brother Carl, who had become a kind of unofficial secretary in Beethoven's dealings with publishers, proposed to the publisher André a ridiculously high fee of 900 florins for three piano sonatas (effectively putting him off, since it was nearly twice the amount charged for the set of three sold to Nägeli), and added: 'My brother does not trouble himself much with such trifles any longer and composes only oratorios, operas, etc.'[2] This information had clearly come from Beethoven himself, and illustrates well the lofty aims he had now adopted. Piano sonatas were mere 'trifles', and Beethoven was wanting to write only the greatest types of music (some years later he expressed a desire to write just operas, oratorios, symphonies, and perhaps string quartets). The oratorio in question was *Christus am Oelberge*, on a subject which as mentioned earlier shows close parallels to Beethoven's own personal sufferings. He composed this during the winter of 1802–3 (the precise chronology is uncertain), in preparation for an *Akademie* the following spring. As for 'operas', this claim has been dismissed by some writers as mere wishful thinking, but it is now clear that Beethoven was indeed making preparations for writing an opera. He regarded opera, like the symphony and string quartet, as a genre that could not be tackled without thorough preparation, and he spent some time during 1801–2 studying Italian word-setting with Salieri. Although he had set Italian words before, notably in his concert aria *Ah! perfido* of 1796, and was by now a celebrated composer of instrumental music, his extraordinary determination to excel in every genre induced him to undergo further study. Under Salieri's tutelage he composed several unaccompanied choruses to Italian words (WoO 99), followed by three exercises in Italian words with orchestral accompaniment: a soprano aria (*No, non turbarti*), a terzet for soprano, tenor and bass (*Tremate*), and a duet for soprano and tenor (*Ne' giorni tuoi felici*). The last of these was being written about the time of Carl's letter of 23 November 1802, and the text is an excerpt from an opera libretto. Thus Beethoven was in a sense writing only oratorios and operas at that time.

Beethoven was at last granted an evening for his long-awaited *Akademie*, which took place on Tuesday 5 April 1803 in the Theater an der Wien. Shortly before then he was also given lodgings at the theatre (along with Carl), evidently with the plan that he would write an opera for performance there in the near future. The concert included four major works – the First and Second Symphonies, *Christus am Oelberge*, and the Third Piano Concerto – all of which apart from the First Symphony were being heard

[2]   Alb-49; BB-113.

for the first time. The Second Symphony had been finished a year earlier, but was probably modified subsequently, for the end of the finale appears to have been significantly extended. The Third Piano Concerto had been written mainly in 1800, but Beethoven now had to finish it off quickly in time for the performance in 1803. The autograph manuscript shows three different shades of ink, with the first two belonging to 1800 and the third entered very hastily shortly before the premiere. Further modifications were made later in 1803 before the work was finally published.

Christus am Oelberge was also finished rather hastily. Ferdinand Ries, who had moved to Vienna at the end of 1802, relates that he was summoned to Beethoven's at 5 a.m. on the day of the concert and found the composer still in bed, writing out the trombone parts that were to be used in the oratorio that evening. As usual there was only one main rehearsal, but it was enormously long, in keeping with the size of the programme. It began at 8 a.m., and by 2.30 everybody was exhausted, as Ries reports. Lichnowsky revived them, however, with large baskets of food and wine, after which they ran through the oratorio once more. The concert then began at 6 p.m., but was so long that in the end some shorter items that had been planned were omitted. The problem that Beethoven had had with finishing the Third Piano Concerto in time is graphically illustrated by Ignaz von Seyfried, who was asked to turn pages for Beethoven at the performance:

> I saw almost nothing but empty leaves; at the most on one page or the other a few Egyptian hieroglyphs wholly unintelligible to me scribbled down to serve as clues for him; for he played nearly all of the solo part from memory since, as was so often the case, he had not had time to put it all down on paper.[3]

Seyfried's account is something of an exaggeration, since the orchestral parts and also some of the piano part were in place in the score, but there were certain passages in which the piano staves were still blank while the orchestra had little or nothing to play, leaving some pages almost empty, while Beethoven's untidy musical handwriting could well have seemed in places to be no more intelligible than Egyptian hieroglyphs to anyone unfamiliar with it. The concert was a great success, for Beethoven made a profit of about 1800 florins – enough to last him for more than a year. The reviews, as usual, were somewhat mixed, for a long, under-rehearsed, and difficult programme of new and advanced music was unlikely to receive a unanimously rapturous reception. All four works, however, received some praise, and the oratorio was regarded as the centrepiece of the occasion. Curiously, it has met with little approval in recent years,

---

[3] TF, p. 329.

although it remained widely admired during Beethoven's lifetime and is a magnificent and highly original work.

Before embarking on the proposed opera, Beethoven set to work on a new symphony, No. 3, no doubt buoyed by the success of the April concert, and he worked intensively on this during the summer months. In fact he was planning at this stage to write two symphonies in quick succession, but no successor to No. 3 emerged for several years, although there are a few sketches for No. 6 from around the end of 1803. The earliest known plan for the Third Symphony appears in the Wielhorsky Sketchbook and was made immediately after the last sketches for the *Prometheus* Variations, around October 1802. This sketch plan shows synopses of the first three movements of what is clearly a grand symphony, and the absence of finale sketches implies that Beethoven had already decided to base the finale on the *Prometheus* theme that he had just been using, a decision he duly carried out. The plan was set aside, however, during the winter months, and taken up again only after his April concert.

Beethoven seems to have intended from the start that this new symphony would be on an unusually grand scale. His Second Symphony was already much longer than No. 1, and longer than any symphony by Haydn or Mozart, but in No. 3 he was aiming for the ultimate, the *non plus ultra*, in symphonic writing, for it is far longer even than No. 2. His ability to work on a larger canvas, already partially developed in his Third Piano Concerto, *Prometheus*, and *Christus am Oelberge*, could now be exploited to the full in the symphonic field. By early autumn the enormous symphony was finished in outline, as is indicated by Beethoven's sketchbook and confirmed by Ries, who reported on 22 October that Beethoven had played it to him recently on the piano. Ries was immediately overwhelmed by the immense power of the work: 'I believe that Heaven and Earth must tremble beneath it when it is performed,' he wrote, adding that Beethoven regarded it as the greatest work he had yet composed.[4] Beethoven did indeed think highly of it, though he was rather more modest when he offered it to Breitkopf & Härtel the following year: 'I believe it will interest the musical public.'[5]

Such a great work needed to be dedicated to a great person, and Beethoven's first thought was Napoleon Bonaparte, who in the years after the French Revolution had risen to become First Consul in France in 1799. Although Austria was at war with France at that time, by 1803 there was an uneasy peace, and it no longer seemed unimaginable to dedicate a work to the leader of the former enemy. Beethoven probably shared the hope that Napoleon could thenceforth help bring Europe to a new era of peace and prosperity based on the ideals of the French Revolution: *liberté*,

---

[4] Alb-71; BB-165.
[5] A-96; BB-188.

égalité, and *fraternité*; and he contemplated moving to Paris, where, as in Vienna, there was a thriving musical scene. A problem immediately arose, however, with the planned dedication, for Prince Lobkowitz wanted it, as well as six months' exclusive use of the work, and was prepared to pay handsomely for the privilege. Beethoven therefore decided instead to use 'Bonaparte' as the title of the symphony, and when his copyist prepared a conducting score it was duly inscribed 'Sinfonia grande intitulata Buonaparte', implying that the symphony was a kind of musical monument to him. But the title is not found among Beethoven's sketches nor on the original manuscript parts used for the first performances.

Beethoven's hopes for Napoleon were soon shattered. It was Ries who brought him the news that Napoleon had proclaimed himself emperor, and Beethoven's immediate response was to attack the autograph score of the symphony, which was lying on his table, as Ries later vividly described:

> He flew into a rage and shouted: 'So he too is nothing more than an ordinary man. Now he also will trample all human rights underfoot, and only pander to his own ambition; he will place himself above everyone else and become a tyrant!' Beethoven went to the table, took hold of the title page at the top, ripped it all the way through, and flung it on the floor.

Beethoven showed far more political awareness than most composers of his time, and had gained strongly anti-tyrannical views in his youth in Bonn. He believed in the ideal of a wise and noble ruler, and had clearly hoped that Napoleon would fulfil such a position after establishing himself as First Consul. He must have had doubts, however, and these were confirmed by Ries's news. He accurately sensed the devastation that would follow in the aftermath of Napoleon's proclamation, and his anger at the news was inevitable. The autograph score of the symphony does not survive, but the copyist's score used at the first performances also betrays Beethoven's anger, for the name 'Buonaparte' on the title page has been erased so heavily that there is a hole in the paper.[6] Yet when his anger had abated, he was willing to restore the name 'Bonaparte', inserting the phrase 'written on Bonaparte' faintly in pencil on the damaged title page and telling Breitkopf & Härtel that the symphony was 'really entitled Bonaparte'. His attitude towards Napoleon and the French remained ambivalent in later years, though it remained more hostile than favourable. The British, however, he much admired, especially their democratic system of government in a two-party state. It is perhaps significant that,

---

[6] The score (complete with hole!) has been published in facsimile: Otto Biba (ed.), *Ludwig van Beethoven: Symphonie Nr. 3, Es-dur, op. 55, 'Eroica': Partitur-Manuskript (Beethovens Handexemplar): Vollständige Faksimile-Ausgabe in Originalformat*, ed. Otto Biba (Vienna: Gesellschaft der Musikfreunde, 1993). Ries's account has been reprinted many times, e.g. in TF, p. 349; WR, p. 68.

immediately before embarking on his 'Bonaparte' Symphony, he had written two sets of variations on patriotic British themes ,'Rule Britannia' and 'God Save the King'.

The first trial performances of the Third Symphony took place at Prince Lobkowitz's palace around the beginning of June 1804, and went appallingly, according to Ries. In the Classical period, symphonies were expected to be grand and imposing public works, but to be based on relatively simple material that could be more or less played at sight. Johann Georg Sulzer wrote in the 1770s: 'Because the symphony must be read directly from the printed music and is not a practice piece (as is a sonata) there should be no difficulties in it that could not be handled by the players and performed crisply.'[7] Beethoven's Third Symphony did not fulfil such expectations, for it has many difficulties such as cross-rhythms and modulations to strange keys that would catch players unawares at the first attempt, as well as tricky and rapid figuration that would require careful practice. Beethoven's lofty ambitions took little heed of such matters, for his aim was to write the greatest symphony yet heard, no matter how difficult, though he always took care to avoid writing anything that was actually unplayable. He made several minor alterations to the music as a result of the trial performances, but not in order to make it easier to play; they were simply the result of his customary determination to make a great work even greater, and to come as close to perfection as he could.

The first public performance did not take place until April 1805, and by this time it had lost its title completely, being announced simply as 'a new grand symphony', neither entitled, nor written on, nor dedicated to, Bonaparte. It received a very mixed reception, with some regarding it as an absolute masterpiece (clearly the view of Lobkowitz and Ries) while others believed it to be diffuse, bizarre, lacking all artistic value, and inordinately long and difficult. A third group took a middle view between these two extremes. Finally, by the time the work appeared in print in October 1806, it had at last acquired the title by which it has become known: *Sinfonia eroica ... composta per festeggiare il sovvenire di un grand Uomo* (Heroic Symphony ... composed to celebrate the memory of a great Man), or more briefly, the *Eroica*. Thus the title may have been Beethoven's response to misguided criticism of the work, as an attempt to help musicians and critics understand and appreciate the underlying concepts of incredible power and grandeur, so that they could approach the work with appropriate expectations. Who the 'great Man' may have been was now deliberately left unspecified: it could be an idealized version of Napoleon, or it could be Prince Lobkowitz, a great musical patron,

---

[7] Johann Georg Sulzer, *Allgemeine Theorie der schönen Kunste* (1771–4), vol. 4, p. 478; quoted from Nancy Kovaleff Baker and Thomas Christensen (eds.), *Aesthetics and the Art of Musical Composition in the German Enlightenment* (Cambridge: Cambridge University Press, 1995), p. 106.

whose name appears as dedicatee immediately after the above title. Most significantly, the 'great Man' could be the composer himself, a heroic figure who had defied Fate and deafness to create an enduring masterpiece that could remain his memorial after his death.

Beethoven had long been attracted by the idea of heroism. His 'heroic' ballet *Prometheus* of 1801 was an early manifestation, and had been immediately followed by a piano sonata (Op. 26) containing a 'Funeral March on the Death of a Hero'. The *Prometheus* Variations (Op. 35) renewed the idea of the ancient hero Prometheus in a different context, while in Beethoven's next significant work Christ was portrayed as the ultimate hero, triumphing over death and saving mankind through his sacrifice on the Cross. The *Eroica* embodies overtones of all these works, with its funeral-march second movement and reference to *Prometheus* in its finale, along with its overall sense of triumph over adversity, and it gradually came to engender an appreciation among the public that composers, too, could be heroes in their own right, a view that helped shape the entire reception of music as an artform in the next two centuries. Almost single-handedly, Beethoven permanently altered public perception of the composer as artist, and his *Eroica* was one of the main works that achieved this change.

Opera

Once Beethoven had completed his *Eroica* he turned his attention to the projected opera for the Theater an der Wien. The artistic director there was Emanuel Schikaneder, who had written the libretto of *Die Zauberflöte* a few years earlier and was now preparing a text for Beethoven entitled *Vestas Feuer* (The Vestal Fire). Beethoven had still not received it when Ries wrote his above-mentioned letter of 22 October 1803, but within a fortnight he commented that he was now beginning to work on it. He made some progress during the next few weeks but rapidly lost interest. He had apparently been given only a section of the text, without any indication of the overall plot, which was based on ancient Rome but had dialogue that was far too colloquial for such a subject. Many composers are somewhat selective about the subjects of their operas, but Beethoven was more choosy than most and rejected countless opera texts during the course of his life. Anything magical, farcical, or lascivious was promptly dismissed. In keeping with his character and outlook, he wanted grand, heroic subjects in which great deeds were done, and once told Gerhard von Breuning (son of his friend Stephan): 'I need something that inspires me; it has to be something moral, edifying. I would never have been able to set to music texts like those Mozart composed.'[8] His preference was for the type of subject popular in France at the time with composers such as Cherubini

---

[8] Gerhard von Breuning, *Memories of Beethoven*, trans. Henry Mins and Maynard Solomon, ed. Maynard Solomon (Cambridge: Cambridge University Press, 1992), p. 97.

and Kreutzer. These operas are often known today as 'rescue operas', since they include some kind of dramatic rescue when all seems lost, although the subject matter itself is quite variable. Cherubini's operas had been introduced to Vienna in 1802, and Beethoven expressed great enthusiasm for them. Thus he was delighted when, around the end of 1803, he found a French libretto that appealed to him in every way. This was *Léonore, ou l'amour conjugal*, a text by Jean-Nicolas Bouilly that had been set by Pierre Gaveaux in 1798. It was now adapted for Beethoven in a German version by Joseph Sonnleithner. The subject concerns Florestan, wrongfully imprisoned for two years in isolation by the wicked Pizarro; Florestan is eventually rescued by his wife Leonore, who has disguised herself as a boy called Fidelio and obtained a job as gaoler's assistant at Pizarro's castle. Bouilly apparently based the plot on events he had actually encountered in Tours during the Reign of Terror in the early 1790s, when political imprisonment was common; the real-life characters are believed to have been Count René Semblançay and his wife Blanche.[9] Such politically sensitive material was regarded as potentially subversive, and Bouilly wisely transferred the setting from Tours to Seville, and from political imprisonment to a mere private dispute between Pizarro and Florestan.

It is easy to see what attracted Beethoven to this subject. He had long hated all forms of tyranny and arbitrary use of power, the kind of oppression that forms the background to the events of the opera. He could also empathize readily with the isolation of Florestan, which recalled his own isolation from society caused by his deafness. A third element that particularly attracted Beethoven was the heroism of Leonore, risking death to save her husband. In fact both partners were heroic in their own ways, for Florestan had been imprisoned for 'daring to speak the truth' (though the details are left vague). Thus the opera could be added to the list of 'heroic' works that Beethoven composed around that time.

What also attracted Beethoven was the fact that Leonore was a loving wife, for he himself had long wished to find such a woman. Coincidentally, he fell deeply in love in the winter of 1804–5 during the composition of *Leonore* (as the early version of the opera is now known). The woman in question was Countess Josephine Deym, who, as mentioned earlier, had come to Beethoven with her sister Therese for piano lessons in May 1799 before marrying Count Deym the following month. The count, however, was nearly thirty years older than Josephine, and died in January 1804. Whether Beethoven perceived Josephine as someone who could rescue him from his isolation in the same way that Leonore rescued Florestan is unclear, but some writers have pointed out that the names Leonore and Josephine have the same four-syllable rhythm in German, so that

---

9 Clive, *Beethoven and his World*, p. 42.

'Josephine' could easily be substituted for 'Leonore' in the opera text (so, too, could 'Beethoven' for 'Florestan' with almost equal ease). Expressions of love between Beethoven and Josephine continued for some months before petering out (see pp. 83–84), and it is possible that Beethoven derived some of his inspiration for his music for the character Leonore from his feelings about Josephine.

Preparations for the opera did not go smoothly. The Theater an der Wien was taken over in February 1804, and the contract for the opera was cancelled before Beethoven had made much progress in its composition. For a time he turned his attention to other new works: the Triple Concerto with violin, cello and piano soloists (a new genre, as he himself observed) and two piano sonatas (Op. 54 and the 'Appassionata', Op. 57). The sonatas were designed as companions to the mighty 'Waldstein' Sonata, which had been composed immediately after *Vestas Feuer*. When *Leonore* was later reinstated in the theatre's plans and Beethoven resumed work on it, he found that it took him longer than expected, owing to his determination to write a complex work of the highest quality and musical interest. The opera was eventually scheduled for 15 October 1805, but there were further delays. Despite Bouilly's and Sonnleithner's efforts to satisfy the censors by changing the location and other details, production of the opera was initially banned and an appeal had to be launched before permission was given. The exceeding difficulty of the music, which was far greater than what the singers and instrumentalists were accustomed to, may also have delayed the performance. Then only a week before the premiere the French army invaded Vienna. Most of the Viennese aristocracy had fled the city on hearing of the approaching army, and the performance took place on 20 November in a nearly empty theatre, with a few French officers forming most of the small audience. After two further performances the opera was withdrawn.

Another problem with *Leonore* was that, for all its fine music, it did not have sufficient dramatic pace, and changes would have to be made if it were to be revived. According to a report by Josef Röckel, who was to be the new Florestan in place of Friedrich Demmer, Beethoven initially refused to change a single note, but was ultimately persuaded by Princess Lichnowsky. Once he had decided to make changes, however, Beethoven set about his task with incredible vigour. He and Stephan von Breuning modified the libretto slightly, while Beethoven himself went through the entire score, making detailed changes in almost every number, altering or removing individual phrases and bars in numerous different places. Altogether over 500 bars were removed, in addition to one whole aria;[10] the first two acts out of the three were merged into one, and the orchestral

---

[10] See Cooper, *Beethoven*, p. 153 (2nd edn, p. 165), for a table showing the relative lengths of each movement in both versions.

introduction to the original Act II was replaced by a short march. The overture was also greatly revised: the 1805 version, now known as *Leonore* No. 2, was tightened structurally to become *Leonore* No. 3, although an additional section resulted in it becoming even longer in its 1806 version. (As mentioned on p. 34, the so-called *Leonore* No. 1 was not composed until 1807.) Considering how many changes there were altogether, they were made with remarkable speed, and the new version was performed on 29 March 1806 and again on 10 April, after which it was set aside once more.

After *Leonore*

The extraordinary speed with which Beethoven worked on the revisions to *Leonore* was maintained throughout the rest of 1806, during which he composed his Fourth Piano Concerto, the three 'Razumovsky' Quartets, the Fourth Symphony and the Violin Concerto. Rarely have so many major masterpieces been composed by one person in a single year. Despite the heroic efforts of the composer at this time, however, none of these works is overtly heroic. The two concertos both exhibit the new expansiveness of Beethoven's middle-period style but are conspicuously gentle, especially in their opening movements, while the symphony is lively and boisterous, with strong rhythms, but substantially shorter than the *Eroica*. Among the instrumental works of 1806, only the first 'Razumovsky' Quartet exudes a strong sense of grandeur and majesty. In this work Beethoven gives to the quartet repertoire what is in some ways equivalent to the *Eroica* and the 'Waldstein' in the genres of symphony and piano sonata, namely a monumental edifice far surpassing anything previously conceived for the medium. All three 'Razumovsky' Quartets, in fact, reflect his 'new way' of composing, and were found exceedingly challenging by early players and listeners: difficult to play and equally difficult to comprehend. Felix Radicati described them simply as 'not music', and Beethoven as 'music-mad', while Beethoven defended them by saying they were for a later age.[11] The incorporation of Russian folk melodies in the first two quartets, in honour of the Russian dedicatee Count Andreas Razumovsky, and Beethoven's skill at thoroughly integrating these melodies into the musical argument were hardly noticed by early critics.

Beethoven spent the latter part of summer 1806 at Lichnowsky's castle in Silesia, but the visit ended abruptly in October. He was asked to play the piano for some visitors, but he had always hated being treated like a circus performer when not in the right mood, and he absolutely refused. When the prince insisted, Beethoven became extremely angry, quickly packed and left the castle at night to catch the very next coach back to

---

[11] TF, p. 409.

Vienna, about 140 miles away. He packed so hastily, in fact, that some of his manuscripts were not given adequate protection and became soaked during a storm on the journey (the water stains are still visible in them!). Back in Vienna he reportedly smashed his bust of Lichnowsky in his anger. This seems entirely plausible, although the comment he is said to have written, that there would be thousands of princes but only one Beethoven, sounds uncharacteristically pompous and is probably fictitious.

One of the composers whose music Beethoven most admired was Muzio Clementi (1752–1832). Clementi had become a successful pianist and composer in London in the late eighteenth century, before entering a partnership in a music publishing and piano-manufacturing business. Similarities between some of Beethoven's piano sonatas and some of Clementi's suggest that Beethoven admired these works particularly. Clementi visited Vienna in 1802 and again in 1804 without making proper contact with Beethoven, for both composers seem to have been wary of initiating an approach; according to Ries, they sometimes even dined at the same table in the restaurant without exchanging more than a brief greeting. In 1807, however, during another visit and after a chance meeting in the street, Beethoven decided to call on Clementi, and they negotiated a deal for the English publication of some of Beethoven's latest works. Although these works were also being published locally by the Bureau des Arts et d'Industrie, Clementi acquired the publication rights for the English-speaking world. The works in question were the Fourth Piano Concerto, the Violin Concerto, the three 'Razumovsky' Quartets, the Fourth Symphony, and the newly composed *Coriolan* Overture. Clementi also managed to persuade Beethoven to make a piano version of the solo part of the Violin Concerto, so that the work could be performed as a piano concerto. Both Clementi and Beethoven were delighted with the agreement, and three works were dispatched at once: the piano concerto, the symphony, and the overture. The other works were sent several months later, once the arrangement of the Violin Concerto had been completed. Unfortunately Napoleon had imposed a blockade on trade between the Continent and England, and as a result the first three were lost in transit after being sent by courier on a roundabout route through Russia. Moreover, the others arrived in London so late that the quartets had long since appeared in Vienna and had been copied by a London publisher, thus preventing Clementi from claiming copyright on them.[12] He was able to do this only for the violin/piano concerto.

The Clementi–Beethoven contract also specified that Beethoven would in due course compose three piano sonatas, or two sonatas and a fantasia,

---

[12] Barry Cooper, 'The Clementi–Beethoven Contract of 1807: A Reinvestigation', in Roberto Illiano, Luca Sala, and Massimiliano Sala (eds.), *Muzio Clementi: Studies and Prospects* (Bologna: Ut Orpheus, 2002), pp. 337–53.

and these works (Opp. 77–9) were duly completed during Clementi's next visit of 1808–10. This time Clementi seems to have brought them back to London personally in 1810, along with some other new works, and they were published so quickly that they appeared even before the Continental editions of them.

The next benefit concert

Beethoven had been hoping to present his latest orchestral compositions at a benefit concert in April 1807, but once again this was prevented. That did not stop him embarking during the summer on two more large-scale works, commissioned by Prince Nikolaus Esterházy and Count Franz von Oppersdorff: the Mass in C and the Fifth Symphony respectively. Esterházy was Haydn's patron, and for a time Haydn wrote one mass for him each year; but Haydn had become too old and infirm to continue composing, and in 1807 Esterházy turned to Beethoven. Like Haydn's late masses, Beethoven's was written to celebrate Princess Esterházy's name-day (Austrians celebrated name-days, on which a saint with the person's name was commemorated, far more than birthdays). As might be expected, Beethoven set the time-honoured Mass text in a highly original way, and with considerable technical difficulties for the performers. As a result, the prince failed to appreciate the work's fine qualities when it was performed in September, describing it as 'unbearably ridiculous and detestable'.[13] Beethoven also had difficulty in finding a willing publisher, though the mass was eventually taken by Breitkopf & Härtel.

The rest of 1807 was devoted mainly to the Fifth Symphony, which Oppersdorff wanted as a successor to No. 4, commissioned by him the previous year and received in February. Beethoven had been contemplating a symphony in C minor as early as the 1780s, when he drafted a two-stave score of the exposition of one (Hess 298), but the earliest ideas for the actual Fifth appear in his sketchbook of 1804. Here the famous opening four-note motif is already in place, as is the variant of it that dominates part of the third movement. But initially Beethoven imagined a minor-key finale, and the present C major finale was conceived much later. The new finale is particularly important for introducing trombones into the symphony orchestra for the first time – previously they had been used only for church music and occasionally opera. Beethoven also added a contrabassoon and piccolo for the movement, thus creating a sense of climactic power that was quite overwhelming. Well aware of its effect, he wrote to Oppersdorff in March 1808: 'The last movement of the symphony is with three trombones and piccolo – though not three

[13] H. C. Robbins Landon, *Beethoven: A Documentary Study* (London: Thames & Hudson, 1970), p. 219.

timpani, but will make more noise than six timpani, and indeed better noise.'[14]

Having completed the Fifth, Beethoven then set to work on a completely different kind of symphony: the *Pastoral*. This had been begun even earlier, in 1803, to judge by the evidence of the sketchbooks, and was perhaps intended as a contrasting companion to the *Eroica*; but it lay undeveloped until he acquired a sketchbook dated '1808' in his hand on the first page, and most of this sketchbook is devoted almost exclusively to this symphony. Beethoven loved the countryside, as he indicated in a letter of 1810, for instance: 'How delighted I shall be to wander for a while through bushes, woods, under trees, plants, rocks. No one can love the country as much as I do.'[15] He managed to conjure up suitable moods in a work that, though thoroughly symphonic and in no way merely pictorial, nevertheless evokes rural imagery throughout. The pastoral quality is indicated both by the title of the work as a whole – *Pastoral-Sinfonie oder Erinnerung an das Landleben, mehr Ausdruck der Empfindung als Malerei* (Pastoral-Symphony or Recollection of Country Life, more expression of feeling than painting) – and by the titles of the individual movements: 'Pleasant, cheerful feelings which awaken on arrival in the country'; 'Scene by the brook'; 'Merry gathering of country people'; 'Thunder, storm'; 'Shepherds' song: glad feelings with thanks to the Godhead after the storm'.[16] Although the symphony appears to have five movements rather than the standard four, the fourth is quite short and could be regarded as a prolonged introduction to the finale; thus the overall structure is not as great a departure from tradition as might appear at first sight. Numerous works with pastoral associations have been composed, both before and since the *Pastoral* Symphony, and they were especially common in the eighteenth century; but no other composer has succeeded in creating such a perfect musical representation of the countryside and the feelings associated with it.

By now Beethoven had a large amount of new music that had never been heard in public, and he was at last granted an evening for a benefit concert on 22 December 1808. Once again this took place in the Theater an der Wien, but on a freezing evening and with an enormous programme that lasted about four hours. It included the Fifth and Sixth Symphonies; the Fourth Piano Concerto, in which Beethoven played the solo part very whimsically, adding many more notes than were in the printed edition; two movements from the Mass in C; the concert aria *Ah! perfido*; a piano extemporization; and to round off the evening, the Choral Fantasia, which combined almost all the forces of the rest of the concert: orchestra, choir,

---

[14] A-166; BB-325.
[15] A-258; BB-442.
[16] These are Beethoven's titles rather than the corrupted versions that appeared in Breitkopf & Härtel's original published version.

vocal soloists, and piano. It was written specially for the occasion, at great speed, shortly before the performance, and the piano introduction had to be improvised by Beethoven on the night; a final version was not worked out until the following year. Although the limited rehearsal time and the difficulty of the music meant that the standard of performance of most of the works left much to be desired, and the ensemble broke down completely at one point in the Fantasia, it was a most extraordinary event, with musicians and audience alike prepared to put up with considerable physical discomfort for the sake of the power, the beauty, and the originality of the music.

Women in Beethoven's life: the 'Immortal Beloved' letter

Beethoven seems to have always had female friends, and many of his compositions are associated with them in some way, either through dedications, through presentation of a manuscript or printed copy, or through works written specially for them. He often fell in love, at least during his twenties, as Wegeler notes: 'In Vienna Beethoven was always involved in a love affair, at least as long as I lived there [1794–6], and sometimes made conquests which could have been very difficult indeed, if not impossible, for many an Adonis.'[1] He also had good relations with many women with whom he did not fall in love. Often they were aristocrats, or pupils, or both.

The list of the main women associated with particular works is quite long, as shown in Table 1, which is arranged in approximate chronological order.

Table 1: *Women associated with particular Beethoven works*

Name	Work	Connection
Antonie von Wolf-Metternich	Dressler Variations, WoO 63	Dedication
Maria von Westerholt	Trio WoO 37	Written for her
Maria von Hatzfeld	Righini Variations, WoO 65	Dedication
Eleonore von Breuning	*Figaro* Variations, WoO 40; two pieces for orphica, WoO 51	Written for her
Two Countesses Thun	Allemandes WoO 42	Copy given to them
Josephine Clary	Mandolin music WoO 43–4; *Ah! perfido*, Op. 65	Written for her
Maria von Lichnowsky	*Judas Maccabaeus* Variations, WoO 45; *Prometheus* (piano arrangement)	Dedications
Babette von Keglevics (later Princess Odescalchi)	Sonata Op. 7; Salieri Variations, WoO 73; Piano Concerto No. 1; Variations Op. 34	Dedications
Anna von Browne	Sonata Op. 10; Variations WoO 71, 76	Dedications

---

[1] WR, p. 43.

Name	Work	Connection
Maria von Thun	Clarinet Trio, Op. 11	Dedication
Josephine von Braun	Sonatas Op. 14; Horn Sonata, Op. 17	Dedications
Maria Theresia of Austria	Septet	Dedication
Henriette Lichnowsky	Rondo Op. 51 No. 2	Dedication
Josephine von Liechtenstein	Sonata Op. 27 No. 1	Dedication
Julie Guicciardi	'Moonlight' Sonata, Op. 27 No. 2	Dedication
Therese von Brunsvik	'Ich denke dein' Variations, WoO 74	Written for and dedicated to her
	Sonata Op. 78	Dedication
Josephine von Brunsvik (later Deym)	'Ich denke dein' Variations, WoO 74	Written for and dedicated to her
	'Andenken', WoO 136; 'An die Hoffnung', Op. 32	Written for her
Marie Bigot	'Appassionata' Sonata, Op. 57	MS given to her
Maria Esterházy	Mass in C	For her name-day
Julie von Breuning	Piano arrangement of Violin Concerto, Op. 61	Dedication
Marie Erdödy	Trios Op. 70; Cello Sonatas Op. 102	Dedications
Caroline Kinsky	Songs Opp. 75, 83, 94	Dedications
Therese Malfatti (?)	*Für Elise*	Written for her
Maximiliane Brentano	Trio WoO 39	Written for her
	Sonata Op. 109	Dedication
Antonie Brentano	'An die Geliebte', WoO 140	MS given to her
	Sonata Op. 111	Intended dedication
	Diabelli Variations	Dedication
Eleonore Pasqualati	*Elegischer Gesang*, Op. 118	In her memory
Elizabeth of Russia	Polonaise, Op. 89	Dedication
Dorothea von Ertmann	Sonata Op. 101	Dedication
Anna Giannatasio	Wedding Song, WoO 105	For her wedding
Cäcilie von Eskeles	'Der edle Mensch', WoO 151	Written for her

The pattern for Beethoven's relationships with women was set in the 1780s, when he fell in love with his pupil Maria von Westerholt, for whose family he is said to have written his Trio for Piano and Wind (WoO 37). The majority of these women were aristocrats, like the Westerholts, and included several countesses

(Wolf-Metternich, Clary, the Thuns, Browne, the Brunsviks, Henriette Lichnowsky, Guicciardi, Erdödy), baronesses (Braun, Pasqualati, Ertmann, Eskeles), princesses (Maria von Lichnowsky, Odescalchi, Liechtenstein, Esterházy, Kinsky), and even empresses (Maria Theresia of Austria, Elizabeth of Russia). This gives some indication of the kind of people with whom Beethoven associated so much of the time, especially during his early years in Vienna. Some were his pupils, while others had given him some favour or sign of friendship that deserved the reward of a dedication.

Some of Beethoven's other music has associations with women. He wrote certain vocal pieces with a particular female singer in mind, notably the songs in his *Egmont* music of 1810, which were designed for Antonie Adamberger. Another work, his Paisiello Variations (WoO 70), was written in 1795 for an unidentified woman friend who had lost a different composer's set of variations on this theme; Beethoven gladly replaced it with a set of his own, allegedly written overnight. His folksong settings were intended more generally for the Scottish women who were the main users of George Thomson's editions of them. Apart from actual women, some of Beethoven's songs also refer to idealized woman, notably 'Adelaide', which praises the beloved in romantic terms. He also had several female friends for whom he did not write any works, such as Nanette Streicher, Bettina (or Bettine) Brentano, Amalie Sebald, and of course his own mother, whom he had once described as his 'best friend'.

For women, as for men, Beethoven believed that 'True friendship can only rest on the connection of similar natures,'[2] and it was his nobility of outlook and that of certain women that so often provided the mutual attraction, whereas base or deceitful women such as his sister-in-law Johanna could never become his friend. In some cases his friendships with women could blossom into love and the possibility of marriage, although sadly this was never fulfilled. He is said to have proposed to Magdalena Willmann as early as about 1795, although this seems unlikely and is at odds with Beethoven's own statement of 1801 that 'for the first time' he thought that marriage might bring him happiness.[3] This statement was made in connection with his next known beloved, Julie Guiccardi, but Beethoven evidently felt that marriage would interfere with his creativity, and he did not pursue the relationship.

[2] Maynard Solomon, 'Beethoven's Tagebuch of 1812–1818', in Alan Tyson (ed.), *Beethoven Studies 3* (Cambridge: Cambridge University Press, 1982), pp. 193–288, entry no. 127.
[3] A-54; BB-70.

Julie meanwhile had fallen in love with Count Gallenberg, and married him in 1803. Yet many years later Beethoven claimed: 'I was much loved by her, and more than her husband ever was.'[4]

Beethoven continued to remain wary of marriage, and when he began seeing Josephine Deym in 1804–5 he wrote: 'When I came to you, it was with the firm resolve not to let a single spark of love be kindled in me. But you have conquered me.'[5] She reciprocated his love, writing, 'A feeling that lies deep in my soul and is incapable of expression made me love you' and 'Only the belief in your inner worth made me love you.'[6] Their love was so strong that Beethoven made some kind of marriage proposal; but Josephine had to refuse for the sake of her children, since as a countess she was liable to lose custody of them if she were to marry a commoner. Thus Beethoven's passionate expressions of love, in which he described her as his 'only beloved', left her unmoved, and they eventually decided that it was better if they stopped seeing each other. There is no confirmed contact known between them after 1807, and she married Baron Christoph von Stackelberg in 1810. Years later, however, her sister Therese expressed her regrets in a poignant diary entry of 1846:

> Beethoven! It seems like a dream that he was the friend, the intimate of our house – a stupendous spirit! Why did not my sister J., as the widow Deym, accept him as her husband? She would have been happier than she was with St[ackelberg]. Maternal love caused her to forego her own happiness.[7]

What Beethoven needed from a woman is perhaps best described by Gerhard von Breuning. Although Breuning was only 13 when Beethoven died, he wrote his recollections as an old man in 1874, having had many years to think them through.

> To make Beethoven happy it would have taken a woman with very special qualities of mind and heart, a woman that it would be hard but possible to find. It would have

---

[4] BKh, vol. 2, p. 365.
[5] A-110; BB-216.
[6] Alb-100 and 102; BB-265 and 250.
[7] See Cooper, *Beethoven*, pp. 147–8 (2nd edn, pp. 158–9), for a recent summary of the relationship, including this quotation. A detailed account of the legal position regarding Josephine's children is given in Marie-Elisabeth Tellenbach, 'Künstler und Ständegesellschaft um 1800: Die Rolle der Vormundschaftsgesetze in Beethovens Beziehung zu Josephine Gräfin Deym', *Vierteljahrschrift für Sozial- und Wirtschaftsgeschichte*, 75 (1988), pp. 253–63.

had to be a woman who understood his flights of genius; who, without encumbering his frequent downswings with additional burdens of everyday affairs, could lead him in a womanly way while protecting him against the heedless outside world and its assaults on him.[8]

Josephine could perhaps have fitted this description, but, like other women he loved, proved to be unattainable, and both she and Beethoven seem to have rejected the prospect of an immoral relationship together. Breuning wrote: 'Beethoven's heart felt love's flames repeatedly, but with the honourable basic idea: "not until I am entitled to call you mine." '[9] Despite many speculative suggestions to the contrary, including unsupported allegations that Beethoven made use of prostitutes during the 1810s or even fathered an illegitimate child, there is no clear evidence that he ever had sexual relations with a woman, although there is no chance of proving that he did not.[10]

In 1809 Beethoven was feeling more stable financially, and asked his friend Ignaz von Gleichenstein to help him look for a wife. Gleichenstein found two eligible young women, Therese and Anna Malfatti, both born in 1792 but not twins (they were born in January and December respectively). In April 1810, while Gleichenstein was wooing Anna, Beethoven indicated he was deeply in love again, apparently with Therese. He set about smartening his appearance, sent for his birth certificate from Bonn, and began planning marriage. But a few months later Stephan von Breuning wrote to Wegeler that these marriage plans had collapsed. It seems that the Malfatti family, though happy to marry their younger daughter to Baron Gleichenstein, were less keen for Therese to marry a mere musician and forbade it.

Beethoven was deeply despondent at the outcome, but he began to recover emotionally when he was visited in late May 1810 by Bettina Brentano and her sister-in-law Antonie, both of whom quickly befriended him. Bettina, who was a friend of the poet Goethe, moved to Berlin later that year and married shortly afterwards. Antonie was already married and normally resided in Frankfurt with her husband Franz, but they had moved temporarily to Vienna to sort out the contents of the house of her father, who had died the previous year. She remained in Vienna until 1812, and when she was feeling ill or depressed Beethoven

---

[8] Breuning, *Memories*, p. 43.
[9] Ibid., p. 44.
[10] On the improbability that Beethoven visited prostitutes, see especially Cooper, *Beethoven*, pp. 223, 277 (2nd edn, pp. 240–1, 298–9).

frequently visited her and improvised comforting music on the piano before leaving in silence. It seems probable that she and Beethoven fell deeply in love during this period. The only direct evidence, however, is a mysterious love letter that Beethoven wrote in July 1812 to an unnamed woman; although Antonie has been proposed as the most likely candidate, many other names have been suggested, and there is no overall consensus among those who have examined the issue most closely.[11] Since the letter is such an extraordinary document and has been the subject of so much controversy, it is given here in full.[12]

16. *Antonie Brentano (1780–1869), wife of Franz Brentano and believed by many to be the intended recipient of Beethoven's famous letter to the 'Immortal Beloved'. Oil painting by Joseph Stieler.*

---

[11] The original suggestion that the woman was Antonie Brentano came from Maynard Solomon; see his *Beethoven*, pp. 158–89, for his full account of the letter and surrounding events.

[12] The translation given here is based partly on Virginia Beahrs, '"My Angel, my All, my Self": A Literal Translation of Beethoven's Letter to the Immortal Beloved', *The Beethoven Newsletter*, 5 (1990), pp. 29, 34–9. Beahrs is one of those who have not accepted Antonie as the woman in question.

6 July, in the morning –
My angel, my all, my self. – Only a few words today, and indeed with pencil – (with yours) only tomorrow is my lodging firmly fixed, what a worthless waste of time on such – why this deep grief, where necessity speaks – can our love endure other than through sacrifices, through not requiring everything. Can you alter it, that you are not completely mine, I not completely yours. O God look into beautiful nature and calm your soul over the inevitable – love demands everything and quite rightly, so it is for me with you, for you with me – only you forget so easily that I must live for myself and for you, were we wholly united, you would feel this painfulness just as little as I. –

My trip was frightful, I arrived here only at 4 o'clock yesterday morning; because they lacked horses, the postal service chose another route, but what a horrible way, at the next to last station they warned me about travelling by night, made me fear a forest, but that only provoked me – and I was mistaken, the coach had to break down on the terrible route, a bottomless, mere country road; without 2 such postilions as I had, I would have been stranded on the way. –

Esterhazy on the other usual route here had the same fate with 8 horses as I had with four. – Yet I had in part some pleasure again, as always, whenever I fortunately overcome something. – Now quickly to interior from exterior, we shall probably see each other soon, even today I cannot convey to you my observations which I made during these few days about my life. Were our hearts always close by each other, I would probably make none such. My heart is full of much to say to you – Oh – there are moments when I find that speech is still nothing at all – cheer up – remain my faithful only treasure, my all, as I for you. The rest the gods must send, what must be and shall be for us. – Your faithful Ludwig. –

Evening on Monday 6 July –
You are suffering, my dearest creature. Just now I notice that letters must be posted very early in the morning, Mondays – Thursdays – the only days on which the post goes from here to K. – You are suffering – Oh wherever I am, you are with me, I talk with myself and you, make it that I can live with you, what a life!!!! thus!!!! without you

– Persecuted by the kindness of people here and there, which I think – I want to deserve just as little as I deserve it – Humility of man towards man – it pains me – and when I regard myself in the framework of the universe, what I am and what is he, whom one calls the Greatest – and yet – herein again is the godly part of the person. I weep when I think that you will probably receive the first news of me only on Saturday – however you love me, I love you even more deeply but – but never hide yourself from me – good night – as a bather I must go to sleep. Oh God – so near! so far! Is not our love a true heavenly edifice? – But also as firm, like the heavenly firmament.

Good morning on 7 July –
Still in bed the ideas press themselves to you, my immortal beloved, now and then happy, then again sad, awaiting fate, if it will hear us. I can live either only wholly with you or not at all [with you], yes I have resolved to wander around so long in the distance, until I can fly into your arms, and can call myself entirely at home with you, can send my soul embraced by you into the realm of the spirits. – Yes unfortunately it must be – you will compose yourself all the more, since you know my faithfulness towards you, never can another possess my heart, never – never – O God, why must one go away from what one so loves, and yet my life in V[ienna] as it is now is a miserable life – Your love makes me the happiest and unhappiest person at once – at my age now I would need some conformity and regularity of life – can this exist in our relationship?

Angel, just now I gather that the post goes every day – and I must therefore close, so that you receive the letter immediately. – Be calm, only through quiet contemplation of our existence can we reach our goal to live together. – Be calm – love me – today – yesterday – What longing with tears for you – you – you – my life – my all – farewell – oh go on loving me – never misjudge the faithful heart of your beloved L.

Ever yours
Ever mine
Ever us

17. *Final page of Beethoven's letter of 6–7 July 1812 to the 'Immortal Beloved'.*

The passages referring to external events are relatively few, but they contain sufficient clues for scholars to have worked out the year, 1812, and that 'K.' refers to the spa town of Karlsbad (now Karlovy Vary, in the Czech Republic). Of Beethoven's acquaintances, the only one known to have been staying there at the right time is Antonie Brentano, which is the main reason why she is still the prime candidate for the woman who has become known as Beethoven's Immortal Beloved, after his own phrase in his second postscript.[13] At that time Beethoven was on holiday in Teplitz (Teplice), about fifty miles from Karlsbad and three days' journey from Vienna. Some passages are almost incoherent or ambiguous, but what Beethoven appears to be saying, with increasing explicitness, is that although he and his beloved will always continue to love each other they will not be able to live together for the present, and so he will have to 'wander ... in the distance'; but it might be possible for them to 'reach our goal to live together' ultimately. This would certainly fit Antonie's situation, for she was attached to her husband and children, and Beethoven was fond of them all (he had recently written a trio for her daughter Maximiliane). If, however, husband Franz were to die before both Antonie and Beethoven, then a union might be possible before Beethoven's soul was sent 'into the realm of the spirits'. Meanwhile his life in Vienna would be miserable – more so than before, since Antonie was about to return to Frankfurt.

It appears that the letter was never sent in the end, for it was found among Beethoven's possessions after his death, with no sign that it had ever been through the post. He must have had doubts about sending it, even though he had carefully concealed the identity of both writer and addressee, in case it were read by someone else, or perhaps misunderstood by the recipient. But he preserved it as a token of his deep love, and put it among his most personal and precious possessions. And he kept his promise to her, 'never can another possess my heart, never – never', for there is no further trace of any amorous relationships during the remaining fifteen years of his life.

Thus Beethoven's longing for a wife remained unfulfilled, despite his many emotional attachments. His awareness of the joys of a happy marriage is reflected in the fact that he twice set Schiller's couplet 'Wer ein holdes Weib errungen / Mische seinen Jubel ein' ('Whoever has gained a lovely wife, let him add his exultation'): in the Ninth Symphony and, paraphrased, in *Fidelio*.

[13] See Chapter Six, 'Myths about Beethoven', for some other possible (and impossible) candidates.

Yet every woman whom he had considered marrying was unavailable – in each case, it seems, for a different reason. Was it bad luck? Was there some psychological block that prevented him falling in love with the right sort of woman? Did he deliberately shun marriage, aware of its pains as well as its joys, despite his apparent efforts to the contrary? There is limitless scope for speculation here, just as there is with the identity of the Immortal Beloved.

There is also scope for speculation about the few factual details in the letter. Why did Beethoven not send the letter? Perhaps he did send it, but in that case why was it returned, what sort of wrapper enclosed it, and why was this not preserved? When did he acquire his beloved's pencil, and why did he not use ink, as in nearly all his other letters? Intensive investigation by numerous scholars, including several whole books on the subject, has thrown light on some details, such as the identity of 'Esterhazy', the routes that he and Beethoven took on their separate journeys between Prague (where they had been staying) and Teplitz, and even the actual text of the letter (one word was misread for years, leading to flawed interpretations). But the controversy over the precise meaning and context of the letter shows no sign of abating, and new studies will probably continue to appear for years.

FOUR

NEW DIRECTIONS (1809–1817)

The annuity contract

Although the year 1809 falls near the middle of Beethoven's 'middle period', and might therefore be expected to be a time of consolidation rather than innovation, the year marked a major turning point in his life in several different ways.[1] By the time he had finished writing the 'Emperor' Concerto early that year, he had completed six symphonies and at least five concertos within the previous decade; yet in the rest of his life such large-scale purely orchestral works largely disappeared from his output, with only three more symphonies (one of which uses voices) and no concertos in the remaining eighteen years. What has sometimes been termed his 'heroic phase' came to an end in 1809 as he turned his attention towards smaller forms, notably lieder, and also embarked that year on a major project, producing a large number of settings of mainly British folksongs.

A second major change was that Beethoven became closely acquainted with Archduke Rudolph (1788–1831), youngest brother of the emperor. Rudolph became the only composition pupil Beethoven ever had: Beethoven normally refused to teach anyone composition, but he seems to have felt compelled to make an exception for a rich, talented, and persuasive archduke. He spent some time preparing teaching materials, which were based partly on his own musical education with Albrechtsberger, and also at this point composed cadenzas for each of his first four piano concertos and the piano version of his Violin Concerto, apparently for Rudolph's use. Rudolph's needs continued to take up much of Beethoven's time for the next fifteen years, a fact that Beethoven sometimes resented, but Rudolph was a very generous patron and

---

[1] See Stephen Rumph, *Beethoven after Napoleon* (Berkeley and Los Angeles: University of California Press, 2004), in which a whole chapter is devoted to this pivotal year, suggesting that Beethoven's life could be divided into two periods rather than the customary three.

received numerous dedications from Beethoven, and there seem to have been no serious disputes between them in all that time.

The political situation also changed dramatically in 1809, for France again invaded Vienna, this time subjecting the city to heavy bombardment and leaving a trail of destruction and desolation. Beethoven was much affected, and for a time found it difficult to concentrate on composition at all. The Austrian government paid for the war through inflation, which had previously been only gradual but was very rapid from 1809, causing havoc with prices and incomes.

Despite the inflation, however, Beethoven's personal financial situation improved greatly at that time, thanks to the generosity of three noblemen who combined to grant him an annuity. The origins of this annuity occurred in late 1808, when he was invited to move to Kassel to become music director to Napoleon's brother Jerome Bonaparte, whom Napoleon had set up as the new 'King of Westphalia'. The proposed salary of 600 ducats (or 2,700 florins) would have been ample for Beethoven, and Kassel was much closer to his native Bonn. He was also to receive 150 ducats in travelling expenses (removal costs), and would have to do little more than conduct at concerts that were not very frequent. He therefore accepted the offer, as he mentioned in a letter of 7 January 1809. His supporters in Vienna, however, were so enthusiastic about his music that they did not want to lose him. Any remaining doubts about his ability had surely been dispelled at his amazing concert of 22 December 1808. Thus plans were set up to make him a rival offer that would be sufficient to induce him to stay. An agreement was drawn up in which Beethoven was to be given 4,000 florins annually, consisting of 1,500 from Rudolph, 700 from Lobkowitz, and 1,800 from Prince Ferdinand Kinsky, who had hitherto shown little involvement in Beethoven's activities but who nevertheless gave the largest contribution towards the annuity. The agreement, dated 1 March 1809, recognized Beethoven's 'extraordinary talents and genius as musician and composer', and aimed to leave him free to compose whatever he wished without having to concern himself with the need to market his compositions to patrons and publishers. It was not even stated explicitly that he was obliged to continue composing at all, though this was understood to be the essence of the agreement. He had only to pledge to remain in Vienna, or some other city under the emperor's rule, and the agreement would continue until he received an appointment of at least equal value. If he did not receive one, the annuity would continue for the rest of his life. It was a most remarkable arrangement, for composers previously had to work for a single patron and be prepared to write specific works on demand, or alternatively chance their arm in the marketplace by writing works that they hoped to sell. Beethoven was therefore uniquely privileged, and it is a mark of his incomparable ability that three patrons were prepared to contribute such large sums of money for his needs. In the event the rampant inflation somewhat undermined the value of the annuity, and some payments were greatly delayed in the confusion, which was made worse by the sudden death of Prince Kinsky in 1812; but the grant was partially revalued in later years, and Beethoven continued to receive payments until his death.

Invasion of Vienna

The war with France reached crisis point in May 1809, and most of the aristocracy left Vienna for the safety of their country retreats. Among them was Archduke Rudolph, and Beethoven quickly composed a farewell piece for him, based on a three-note motif to the syllables 'Le-be wohl' (Farewell). He inscribed the manuscript with a touching dedication: 'The Farewell: Vienna, 4 May 1809 on the departure of His Imperial Highness the esteemed Archduke Rudolph'. Some months later he added two further movements, 'Absence' and 'The Return', to form a three-movement sonata, in anticipation of Rudolph's return to Vienna, which did not take place until the following January. This was the only one of Beethoven's 35 piano sonatas to have an explicit biographical connection, and the inscriptions on the music clearly meant much to him, for he was angry when Breitkopf & Härtel published the sonata without the inscriptions and with the title translated into French as 'Les adieux', which, as he pointed out, means something quite different and much less personal.

The French had soon reached the gates of the city, and they bombarded it relentlessly during the night of 11–12 May. Beethoven is reported to have spent the night in a cellar at his brother's house, covering his ears with pillows to protect his weak hearing. The next few weeks were almost as bad, with the citizens suffering great deprivation during the occupation. He wrote to Breitkopf & Härtel on 26 July: 'We have recently been experiencing really concentrated misery. I can tell you that since 4 May I have brought to the world little coherent work, practically just a fragment here and there ... What a destructive, disorderly life is here around me, nothing but drums, cannons, human misery in every form.'[2] Beethoven had been deeply affected by the disruption to his everyday life, and by his inability to move from the city to some outlying village for the summer as normal. A French officer, Baron de Trémont, called on him a few times during the occupation and found that his rooms, which were habitually untidy, were even more so than usual:

> Picture to yourself the dirtiest, most disorderly place imaginable
> – blotches of moisture covered the ceiling; an oldish grand piano,
> on which the dust disputed the place with various pieces of

---

[2] A-220; BB-392.

printed and manuscript music; under the piano (I do not exaggerate) an unemptied chamber pot ... The chairs, mostly cane-seated, were covered with plates bearing the remains of last night's supper, and with clothing etc.[3]

Beethoven was indeed living a disorderly life as he had claimed, and his sketchbook confirms that he composed nothing of significance during this period. His work did not return to normal until about August, after an armistice with France had been signed in July. Meanwhile he spent some time studying scores and some of the great works of literature, an activity that was one of his favourite pastimes. He engrossed himself in the works of Euripides, Goethe, Schiller, Homer, and others, and asked Breitkopf & Härtel to send him music by Mozart, Haydn, and Bach. He appears to have been attempting to forge a new path based on deeper learning and understanding – another major turning point in his activity, though it did not immediately have any obvious effect on his composition. During the latter part of 1809 he composed several works: a string quartet (Op. 74, the so-called 'Harp' Quartet), whose relative normality compared with his recent orchestral works could be seen as a reaction against all the disruption of the previous few months; several songs, some with Italian texts and some in German; and the remaining piano works that he had promised Clementi two years earlier.

Folksong settings

It was at this time that Beethoven embarked on a project instigated by a Scotsman, George Thomson of Edinburgh (1757–1851): the composition of settings of folksong melodies. During the eighteenth century there had arisen in Britain a fascination for Scottish folksong, with collections of poems and/or tunes being published with increasing frequency. Gradually enthusiasm for the genre spread to other countries: Ireland, Wales, and later Germany, where the poet Johann Gottfried Herder was particularly active. This is perhaps the only occasion on which Scotland has led the way in the development of a musical genre of international importance. The Scottish tunes were often published with accompaniments for harpsichord – later for piano – provided by various composers, mostly British. Thomson aimed to produce a bigger, purer, and more elaborate collection than any preceding one, and engaged some of the most prominent composers in Europe to provide accompaniments: Pleyel, Kozeluch, and even Haydn. He also asked for the addition of preludes and postludes rather than just accompaniments, and these settings were to be written not just for piano but with optional parts for violin and cello too. When Haydn finally gave up composing these settings, Thomson naturally turned to Beethoven,

---

[3] Sonneck (ed.), *Impressions*, p. 70.

writing to him as early as 1803; but the project did not eventually start until 1809. In September that year Thomson sent Beethoven forty-three melodies, mainly Irish and Welsh, since he had already published several Scottish collections. Beethoven had started making settings by the time he wrote to Thomson in November, although he did not finally send this batch until the following July, by which time he had set ten more melodies sent by Thomson, making a collection of fifty-three. Because of Napoleon's embargo on trade between Britain and the Continent, however, Beethoven had to send three copies, by different routes, hoping that at least one would reach its destination. The first one did not arrive until two years later, having travelled on a circuitous route via Malta. Despite these practical difficulties, Beethoven continued making further settings intermittently until 1820, by which time he had sent Thomson a total of 177 (and written two more not sent to Thomson), including several of melodies from various Continental countries.

Beethoven's settings have not always been fully appreciated, but they are quite extraordinary, for he thoroughly transformed the genre, surpassing all his predecessors in many different ways. In his preludes, instead of writing a four-square melody based on the opening phrase of the tune and closing in a typical Classical cadence, as other composers had done, he most often singles out an important motif from the tune and develops it symphonically, often in irregular phrase lengths, until the tune eventually bursts forth like a flower from its bud, almost invariably without any break in the rhythmic momentum. His settings also typically contain far more energetic accompaniments than those of his predecessors, with vigorous semiquaver figures common, rather than just plain chords. For the string parts he often wrote antiphonal motifs for violin and cello (what Thomson described as 'delicious little conversations' between them), another innovation; and he sometimes inserted one or two bars of interlude in the middle of a stanza, another new feature that pleased Thomson. At the end of each stanza, as at the end of the prelude, Beethoven normally kept up the momentum through continued rhythmic activity; he also departed from all previous practice by composing a postlude that ran straight on into the next stanza, with a different version of the postlude to be played after the final stanza. Thus throughout each setting there is continuous forward momentum to a single culmination at the end, whereas in previous settings there was usually a point of repose at the end of the prelude, again at the end of each stanza, often also in the middle of each stanza, and again at the end of each rendition of the postlude, resulting in a rather disjointed effect and little overall cohesion.

Beethoven's settings exhibit several other innovations, including unprecedented sensitivity to the words, where these were provided for him. If they were not provided, however, he was happy to create purely abstract settings based on the musical material, aware that many folk tunes could be sung to more than one set of words, so that detailed word-painting would not always be appropriate. Thomson then skilfully matched Beethoven's settings with appropriate poems by Robert Burns, Walter Scott, and others.

Although some of the settings proved technically too difficult for Thomson's intended market of female amateurs, so that Beethoven occasionally had to supply replacement settings that were more suitable, Thomson was thrilled with them in every other way, writing to a friend in 1812:

> They are exquisitely beautiful, and when an opportunity offers of playing them with any musical friends, we repeat them ten times in a night con amore, and still find new beauties to admire, for the composition of the Ritornelles [preludes and postludes] & of the harmony is as much superior to the every day works we meet with, as the Dramas of Shakespeare transcend those of ordinary Compilers for the stage.[4]

Goethe

One of the reasons why Beethoven took longer than expected to complete his first batch of folksong settings was that he was asked to write incidental music for Goethe's play *Egmont* in early 1810. Beethoven loved Goethe's works and had already set several of his poems as songs; he had even begun a setting of one of the songs from *Egmont* itself. Thus he readily agreed to the task, not having previously written any significant incidental music for plays. The play concerns Count Egmont as honest and fearless leader of the Dutch people in the Spanish-occupied Netherlands in the sixteenth century. When a new and repressive regent, the Duke of Alva, arrives, Egmont is arrested and eventually executed, but not before he has had a vision of ultimate victory for a free Netherlands. The focus on oppression and freedom was bound to appeal to Beethoven; meanwhile the obvious similarities with the recent French invasion of Vienna would have been patent to all. Beethoven eagerly wrote the four entr'actes and five other numbers, adding a particularly fine and evocative overture. Both the overture and the incidental music reveal his deep understanding of Goethe's text and his own skill in creating music that matches it so perfectly. The music was not ready for the first performance of the new production, on 24 May 1810, but it was finally heard at the fourth performance on 15 June.

It was while Beethoven was finishing his *Egmont* music that he first met Goethe's friend Bettina Brentano. Bettina wrote a long letter to Goethe

---

[4] Quoted from Barry Cooper, *Beethoven's Folksong Settings* (Oxford: Clarendon Press, 1994), p. 203; this book gives a detailed account of the history and the style of the settings.

on 28 May, describing her meetings with Beethoven. Although she had a vivid imagination and her testimony is unreliable, it is clear that she and Beethoven quickly became close friends, and some believe they even fell in love. She left Vienna for Berlin shortly afterwards, and married the poet Achim von Arnim on 11 March 1811; but a month before the wedding Beethoven wrote to her (the letter is dated 10 February) expressing warm feelings for her and wishing her every blessing in her marriage.[5] Towards the end of the letter he even intermittently used the intimate *du* for 'you', which he had not done in his love letters to Josephine Deym a few years earlier (but which he did in his letter to the Immortal Beloved in 1812). The letter mentions his enormous admiration for Goethe and indicates Beethoven's intention to write to the poet direct. He duly did this in April, mentioning Bettina and also promising a copy of his music for *Egmont*, which he asked the publishers Breitkopf & Härtel to send direct to Goethe. Goethe replied in June from Karlsbad, where he was on holiday, expressing his admiration for Beethoven's 'extraordinary talents'; he had heard several good reports about the *Egmont* music, and indicated that he would try to arrange a production of both play and music after returning to his home in Weimar. Thus was forged a link between the two greatest German artists of the time, if not of all time, and Beethoven's *Egmont* music was duly performed in Weimar with Goethe's play in 1814. By that time the two men had actually met and Beethoven had begun a setting of two more Goethe poems (see below).

Visits to Bohemia and Linz

Beethoven spent the autumn and winter of 1810–11 composing several more works, including the String Quartet in F minor, Op. 95, the 'Archduke' Trio, and three songs with texts by Goethe, Op. 83. For much of the time, however, he was unwell, and on medical advice he decided to spend the next summer at Teplitz, where he arrived on 4 August. Like Karlsbad, Teplitz was a spa town in northern Bohemia where many wealthy and cultured people from both Saxony and Prussia to the north and Prague and Vienna to the south stayed during the summer, and was famous for the healing properties of its hot springs. Thus it offered the double attraction of stimulating company and a chance of recovery from his chronic digestive illnesses. Beethoven took advantage of both, meeting several interesting people despite the social impediment of his deafness, and quickly feeling in much better health. It was here that he completed two one-act singspiels that had been commissioned for the opening of a new theatre in Pest: *König Stephan* and *Die Ruinen von Athen*. According to Beethoven he was given the texts only as he was about to set out for

---

[5] Two other letters from Beethoven to Bettina are believed by most people to be the result of her imagination, and survive only in 'copies' that she claimed to have made.

Teplitz, but the size of the works and the extent of the sketches, coupled with the absence of any other compositions immediately following the 'Archduke' Trio of March 1811, indicate that he must have spent several months on the two works. They were meant to be performed in October that year, but the premieres had to be postponed till the following February, even though Beethoven had for once completed his contribution in good time. Both works – especially *Die Ruinen von Athen* – contain some fine music; but their underlying subject, the glorification of culture in Pest, is so closely bound up with their origins as a celebration of a new theatre there that they have had little success elsewhere.

The visit to Teplitz was so successful that, again on medical advice, he returned there the following summer, after composing his Seventh Symphony and making a start on the Eighth. This second visit has been subjected to intense scrutiny because of Beethoven's letter to the Immortal Beloved (see pp. 86–88). Yet this letter was in some ways only one small incident in his extended stay in Bohemia. He left Vienna probably on 29 June 1812, and spent three nights in Prague (1–4 July). While there he attempted to sort out some problems with his annuity from Prince Kinsky, since a fivefold devaluation of the florin in 1811 meant that Beethoven was now being paid less than he felt entitled to. Meanwhile Franz and Antonie Brentano arrived in Prague on 3 July. They left for Karlsbad the next day, while Beethoven left for Teplitz. His journey was greatly delayed by bad weather, and he did not arrive until 4 o'clock on the Sunday morning (5 July).

A few days later Beethoven was lamenting in his letters that there were fewer visitors to Teplitz than the previous year, and not such interesting ones. However, Goethe arrived on 14 July and he finally met Beethoven five days later. Thereafter they were in daily contact for about a week. The day after they first met, they visited nearby Bilin together, and the following day they spent the evening together, with Beethoven playing the piano for Goethe. Goethe's views of Beethoven are most interesting and reveal acute perception. On the day they first met, Goethe wrote: 'A more self-contained, energetic, sincere artist I never saw.' Later he observed: 'His talent amazed me; but unfortunately he is an utterly untamed personality, who may really be not at all wrong in finding the world detestable, but surely does not thereby make it more enjoyable either for himself or for others.'[6] Beethoven often had difficulty in accepting that not everyone would uphold high moral standards; but, as Goethe observed, it certainly did not help if he went around criticizing them for not doing so. What the two great artists discussed together is difficult to establish, but it seems that they agreed that Goethe would adapt his *Faust* for Beethoven to set as an opera, which, as Beethoven later stated, was the

---

[6] TF, pp. 536–7 (translation altered).

one work that he would most like to have composed; but this never came about.

After another week Beethoven left Teplitz, again on the instructions of his doctor, and moved to Karlsbad. There he stayed in the same house as the Brentanos, and on 8 August they all moved on to Franzensbad (now Františkovy Lázně), where they again shared lodgings. This was probably the last place in which they saw each other, for Beethoven later moved back to Karlsbad (where Goethe was by that time) and then back to Teplitz, as his doctor repeatedly tried to find him the best place for a cure. Yet soon after his return to Teplitz he was so unwell that he had to stay in bed for several days, blaming food poisoning and a walk in the fog for his condition.

Once Beethoven had recovered sufficiently from his illness, he set off from Teplitz to see his brother Johann, who had set up as a pharmacist in Linz in 1808 and had been very successful there. Beethoven found Johann living intimately with his housekeeper Therese Obermayer, and immediately determined to put a stop to the relationship. He had no right to do so, of course, but his desire that others should live up to his standards took over again, and he felt duty-bound to protect his brother from a woman who already had an illegitimate daughter, Amalie Waldmann. Beethoven no doubt recalled the fate of his other brother Carl, whose wife Johanna was clearly an unworthy woman (she had become pregnant with their son Karl some months before their marriage in 1806), and who had recently brought disgrace on the family name through a criminal conviction in 1811 for theft of some pearls that had been entrusted to her (and for trying to cover her traces by faking a burglary at her house). The prospect of having a second unworthy sister-in-law, or alternatively seeing his brother in an illicit relationship, was something Beethoven clearly found hard to bear, and he made every effort to have Therese evicted from Johann's house. He may even have visited Linz specifically for this purpose, as Thayer argues. He spoke to the local bishop and even involved the police in his efforts to end the relationship. Johann felt forced to marry Therese to end all dispute, and the wedding took place on 8 November.

While in Linz Beethoven completed his Eighth Symphony, a strikingly cheerful and humorous work, but it clearly did not match his mood during this period. He returned to Vienna in November, more despondent than usual. The Brentanos departed for Frankfurt that month, never to return, and Beethoven had resolved not to see his Immortal Beloved again (whether or not she was Antonie). He had failed completely to persuade Johann to renounce Therese. Meanwhile his other brother, Carl, had fallen ill with tuberculosis, and from this time until Carl's death in 1815 Beethoven expended large sums of money to support Carl and his family during the illness. He was also owed money by both Lobkowitz, who was experiencing financial difficulties, and Kinsky, who had not revalued the amount he was paying Beethoven when he died suddenly from an accident in November. The matter was not settled by Kinsky's heirs until January 1815. Thus Beethoven was more than usually overwhelmed with the cares of the world in late 1812, as he made strenuous efforts to obtain what was rightfully his. Although he managed to complete his Violin Sonata in G (Op. 96) for a visit of the violinist Pierre Rode in December, his creativity seems to have suffered considerably in the months after the completion of the Eighth Symphony, with a projected Ninth being abandoned for the moment. About this time, too, he began jotting his thoughts down in a notebook known as his Tagebuch, which he continued to use intermittently for some six years (see 'Beethoven's beliefs and attitudes: the Tagebuch', pp. 107–114). His despondency with the world is evident in the very first entry, where he tells himself: 'For you there is no longer any happiness except in yourself in your art.'[7]

Into the limelight and out again

Several entries early in his Tagebuch suggest that Beethoven was wanting to make changes to his life, to break out and do something afresh. By implication this also meant composing something quite different, rather than yet another symphony. He refers to a 'long journey', doing great deeds, and not continuing his everyday existence. Around March 1813, still remembering his recent time with Goethe, he began setting the poems 'Meeresstille' and 'Glückliche Fahrt' (Calm Sea and Prosperous Voyage) as a short choral piece, using some highly effective word-painting, but he found himself unable to move forward on this, just like the becalmed ship in Goethe's poem, and the setting was not completed for over two years. Meanwhile he finally found a way of advancing his art in the most unlikely manner, by composing a battle piece. Music depicting battles was plentiful at the time, but most of it was mediocre in quality, with obvious pictorial devices and little musical interest. The idea of showing how such a piece could and should be written came as a result of the victory of the Duke of Wellington at Vitoria in Spain against the occupying French army, in June 1813. When news reached Vienna there was great jubilation and optimism that the French forces might at last be driven back, especially after their appalling losses the previous winter in an ill-fated invasion of Russia. The inventor Johann Maelzel was in Vienna at the time, and had invented a mechanical organ known as a panharmonicon. Beethoven composed a Victory Symphony for this instrument, to celebrate Wellington's victory, and then proceeded to arrange the work for full orchestra. He then added an orchestral movement depicting the actual battle in very vivid terms, calling the work *Wellingtons Sieg* (Wellington's Victory; it is often known as the 'Battle

---

[7] Solomon, 'Beethoven's Tagebuch', p. 212 (translation altered).

Symphony'). The French and English sides are represented by a traditional French and English melody respectively (though the French melody is now sung in Britain to the rather inappropriate words 'For he's a jolly good fellow'). Cannon-fire, played by large bass drums, is heard from both sides, occurring seemingly at random (but cunningly measured out irregularly by Beethoven), and the French cannons are gradually silenced. The Victory Symphony makes much use of the tune of 'God Save the King', to confirm who the victors are.

Wellingtons Sieg is ostentatiously popular in style, and has often been condemned by musical purists, but it dwarfs all previous attempts at battle music in its sophistication, originality, and masterly portrayal of events. It was enormously successful when it was premiered in Vienna, and Maelzel proposed that he and Beethoven should take the work to London and present it there, in the hopes of making a fortune. They soon quarrelled, however, and the trip to London did not take place. Nevertheless when the work was performed there it again met with great enthusiasm from the audience.

Apart from the ear-trumpets mentioned earlier, which Maelzel devised to assist Beethoven's weak hearing, another of his inventions was the metronome, the device by which he is best remembered today. Beethoven had previously lamented that he could never indicate speeds properly with vague terms like 'allegro' and 'largo'. Thus he was delighted with Maelzel's invention and was the first major composer to use it. He found it quite tiresome to work out and write down the correct figure for each movement, and he occasionally made a mistake in the process, which resulted in a wrong figure being handed down to posterity. But he nevertheless provided metronome marks for many of his more important works, including all his symphonies.

The public premiere of both *Wellingtons Sieg* and the Seventh Symphony took place at a highly successful charity concert on 8 December 1813, and the event was repeated four days later. Beethoven was then granted two benefit concerts of his own, which resulted in further successful performances and a sizeable income for him. With these performances he reached the zenith of his popularity and prosperity. He could still hear well enough to conduct these works, and Louis Spohr left an account of Beethoven's conducting style, in which he flung his arms about, crouched down, or sprang up high, in efforts to convey the feeling of the music to the orchestra. Such motions, though fairly normal today, caused considerable amusement since they were evidently a novelty at a time when conductors usually did little more than keep time (if there was a conductor at all – often performances were directed by the leader of the violins).

The success of these concerts induced the court theatre directors to propose a revival of *Fidelio*. Beethoven agreed, provided he were allowed to make substantial revisions. A new librettist was called on, Georg

Friedrich Treitschke, who thus became the fourth librettist after Bouilly, Sonnleithner, and Breuning. Beethoven also wrote a fourth overture, now known as the *Fidelio* Overture, rejecting all three *Leonore* overtures. Treitschke did a masterly job at revising the libretto, showing a keen sense of drama and characterization, and Beethoven was very pleased. Particularly successful was the second half of Florestan's aria, 'Und spür' ich nicht linde', which was entirely new and portrays Florestan's vision of an angel leading him to freedom in heaven – a message with powerful political overtones. Treitschke later described how this music was composed:

> Beethoven came to me about seven o'clock in the evening. After we had discussed other things, he asked how matters stood with the aria. It was just finished; I handed it to him. He read, ran up and down the room, muttered, growled, as was his habit instead of singing – and tore open the piano. My wife had often vainly begged him to play; today he placed the text in front of him and began wonderful improvisations, which unfortunately no magic could hold fast. Out of them he seemed to conjure the motif of the aria. The hours passed, but Beethoven improvised on. Supper, which he had intended to share with us, was served, but he did not let himself be disturbed. It was late when he embraced me, and declining the meal, he hurried home. The next day the admirable composition was finished.[8]

In his earlier years Beethoven frequently composed at the piano, probably somewhat along these lines, but such composing was rarely overheard by others and even more rarely reported. In later years he took to more cerebral methods of composition when his deafness became too bad, but it clearly did not impede him that evening. Beethoven's sketchbook supports Treitschke's account, for it shows that this aria was composed at a very late stage, after both the finales in the opera, and the sketches for it are in a different ink from the surrounding sketches, suggesting that they were composed away from home. They appear to have been jotted down very hurriedly, and represent early stages in the compositional process; the later stages of sketching, worked out 'the next day', are unfortunately lost.[9] The new version of the opera received its premiere on 23 May 1814 (though the overture was still not ready and a different one was substituted); and after a few further revisions it reached its final form at a performance on 18 July.

---

[8] TF, pp. 572–3.
[9] See Barry Cooper, 'The Composition of "Und spür' ich" in Beethoven's *Fidelio*', *The Music Review*, 47 (1986–7), pp. 231–7, for a fuller account of the sketches and their interpretation.

18. *Engraving by V. R. Grüner, 1815, of a scene from*
Fidelio, *showing the moment where Leonore reveals her*
identity and intervenes to prevent Pizarro murdering her
husband Florestan, with the dramatic words 'First kill
his wife!'.

By this time Napoleon had been roundly defeated, and there was great
rejoicing in Vienna. Beethoven contributed several occasional works
during this period, of which the most substantial is the grand cantata *Der
glorreiche Augenblick* (The Glorious Moment). This was composed for
performance during the Congress of Vienna, a meeting of numerous
heads of state during the autumn and winter of 1814–15 to decide on the
shape of Europe after the Napoleonic wars. The congress was marked by
lavish entertainments and parties, and although Beethoven remained
largely on the fringes his cantata was performed successfully on three
occasions. It has failed to make much impact outside its original context,
however, and is now almost completely neglected.

During 1815 Beethoven seems to have withdrawn, whether deliberately
or merely as a result of circumstances, from the prominent position he
had occupied the previous year. He began a new piano concerto, but
quickly laid it aside to concentrate on more private chamber works in
which a new style is often apparent. This late style is difficult to
characterize precisely, but it involves more complex forms, more intricate
and polyphonic part-writing, and an even greater sophistication in the

handling of themes and motifs. It is truly music for connoisseurs. The first works where this style is manifest are the two Cello Sonatas Op. 102 and the Piano Sonata Op. 101, plus the song cycle *An die ferne Geliebte* (To the Distant Beloved). This last work, composed in April 1816, has been seen by many as a belated response to Beethoven's own amorous encounter with his Immortal Beloved, as well as the first true *Liederkreis* or song cycle, a genre that was shortly to be taken up with enthusiasm by composers such as Schubert and Schumann. As in many of his late works, Beethoven here combined surface simplicity and directness of appeal with an underlying motivic, tonal, and structural complexity, plus an extraordinary emotional depth that suggests an autobiographical element.

At this time Beethoven was once again beset with serious family problems. His brother Carl had finally died on 15 November 1815, having made a will in which he initially nominated his wife Johanna and Beethoven as co-guardians of his nine-year-old son Karl but altered the wording to make Beethoven sole guardian when Beethoven objected to Johanna. Carl was then induced behind Beethoven's back to add a supplement or codicil reinstating Johanna; and although he agreed to reverse this, the lawyer could not be found at the crucial moment, before Carl died early the next morning. The result was a protracted legal struggle that went first one way and then the other. Beethoven claimed that Johanna was unsuitable as she lacked the necessary education to be guardian of an older boy and was also legally ineligible because of her criminal conviction of 1811; he also stated that Carl's codicil reinstating Johanna was signed under pressure from her, and did not reflect Carl's true intentions. It may be observed in support of this that the original will and Carl's alteration are both in his hand, but the codicil was drafted and written out by someone else and merely signed by Carl, who may on his deathbed have been physically and mentally too weak to resist his wife's pressure to do so. The legal body, the *Landrecht*, ruled initially in Johanna's favour, with Karl continuing to live with her, but they then reversed their decision in January 1816 and Karl was placed in a boarding school run by Cajetan Giannatasio. Beethoven's deep love for Karl was reflected in enormous concern over his welfare at Giannatasio's, and he was prepared to pay whatever was necessary to obtain the best education, including a suitable piano teacher. He continued to sacrifice much time and money for the sake of Karl for the rest of his life. The guardianship dispute, however, was to surface again in 1818.

On 15 October 1816 Beethoven fell ill with an 'inflammatory fever'. His health had long been precarious, with bouts of mild illness (mostly digestive) intermittently relieved by visits to local spas (Baden and Heiligenstadt) or, in 1811 and 1812, spas in Bohemia. This time, however, his illness, though not life-threatening, left him debilitated and virtually unable to compose for a whole year, with clear signs of chronic fatigue

19. *Beethoven's nephew Karl (1806–58) in cadet's uniform. Unsigned miniature.*

syndrome.[10] He managed to struggle to the end of the Piano Sonata Op. 101, the autograph of which is dated November 1816, but the essential composing of it had already been achieved before his illness. Thereafter he managed to complete only a few folksong settings (which required less effort) and one or two very minor works before the end of 1817.

He was still struggling to recover his strength that summer when he received a letter from Ferdinand Ries on behalf of the Philharmonic Society of London (where Ries was now living), inviting him to come to England for the early months of 1818 and bring two new symphonies for performance in London. The terms were generous, and Beethoven knew that Haydn had greatly profited from his two visits to England in the 1790s. Thus he happily accepted the proposal on 9 July and began composing the first of the two new symphonies. There were insuperable difficulties, however. Beethoven could not bear to leave his nephew in the company of Johanna for such a long period, and therefore demanded payment for a travelling companion too (obviously Karl), which the

---

[10] Some writers have attempted to attribute Beethoven's decline in productivity at this time to other causes, but Beethoven himself repeatedly and convincingly emphasized that his illness of October 1816 was to blame: see Cooper, *Beethoven*, p. 254 (2nd edn, p. 273).

society may have been reluctant to meet. More seriously, although the earliest sketches clearly intended for what became his Ninth Symphony date from the latter part of 1817, they are relatively few and undeveloped, and the only recognizable ones are for the first movement. Thus he could not possibly have brought one new symphony, let alone two, with him to London in early 1818 on the basis of what he sketched at that time. Consequently he remained in Vienna that winter.

This dramatic slow-down in his speed of composition is a clear indication of the enormous effort he habitually put into writing major works, an effort that in turn required much energy and a certain level of health. Without this energy he could achieve little. Much of 1817, therefore, was spent with domestic cares, concerning which he wrote many letters to his old friend Nanette Streicher, since he was now seriously considering the possibility of having Karl live at home with instruction from a personal tutor. Beethoven also spent time reading his favourite authors, and about that time he copied several choice passages into his Tagebuch. This document reveals so much about his inner life that it deserves to be examined in some detail in a separate section.

Beethoven's beliefs and attitudes: the Tagebuch

Beethoven compiled his Tagebuch during the period 1812–18. The original document is lost, but fortunately a copy was made by Anton Gräffer shortly after Beethoven's death. A modern edition and translation of this copy was published in 1982 by Maynard Solomon,[1] who divided the entries into 171 numbers, some of which are compound entries. His numbering is retained here (with the prefix T-). The entries have a great diversity of topics. Some are purely mundane, while others relate to Beethoven's personal relationships and especially his concern for his nephew. Many, however, reflect his thoughts about his circumstances or his beliefs and attitudes, and there are frequent quotations from literature, selected apparently for the significance of their content as reflections of his own thoughts. Thus the Tagebuch entries offer a vital window into Beethoven's spiritual world and provide an excellent starting point for understanding it.

Literary quotations in the Tagebuch are from a variety of sources. Authors from classical antiquity represented by either quotation, paraphrase, or reference include Homer (both *The Iliad* and *The Odyssey*), Hesiod, Ovid, Pliny, and Plutarch. Of these, Beethoven had particular admiration for Homer, while he seems to have regarded Plutarch's *Lives*, which records the biographies of many great men of antiquity, as an inspiration for his own life. Curiously, there are no direct references to, or quotations from, the Bible. Instead Beethoven copied down several extended passages derived from ancient Indian religion, filtered through such European writers as Johann Friedrich Kleuker and Sir William Jones. Also surprisingly absent are any references to Goethe, whom Beethoven greatly admired; and the only reference to Shakespeare, whom he equally admired, is a brief quotation from someone who had compared Michelangelo, Shakespeare, and Beethoven as parallel examples in different art forms. Friedrich Schiller, Johann Gottfried Herder, and Immanuel Kant, however, are represented by several quotations, while there is also a reference to the Spanish writer Pedro Calderón. The final entry is from Christian Sturm's

---

[1] Solomon, 'Beethoven's Tagebuch'; a revised version of this is in Solomon's *Beethoven Essays* (Cambridge, MA: Harvard University Press, 1988). There is also a German edition by Sieghard Brandenburg. The present translations sometimes differ slightly from those of Solomon.

Betrachtungen über die Werke Gottes (Reflections on the Works of God), an extremely popular religious book at the time, providing reflections for every day of the year based on observations in nature that lead to the praise of God. Beethoven owned a copy of this book, and his 117 markings of particular passages show that he read it avidly. His *Pastoral* Symphony shows something of the same approach as Sturm's, since it concludes with shepherds giving 'thanks to the Godhead' after depictions of nature.

Deep-seated religion was in fact at the heart of Beethoven's outlook. Although he showed neither a Protestant devotion to the Bible nor a Catholic devotion to the Church (despite his Catholic background), he had profound religious faith in God, and tried to impart this to his nephew Karl; at a court hearing Karl revealed that they prayed together twice daily. Beethoven's view of the nature of God became somewhat coloured by Indian religion during the 1810s, as is indicated by several quotations in the Tagebuch, but all of these quotations are consistent with traditional Christian teaching, as in the following examples:

> O Godhead … you are the true, eternally blessed, unchangeable light of all time and space. Your wisdom perceives a thousand and several thousand laws, and yet you act ever freely and to your honour. You existed before everything that we perceive. To you, praise and adoration. You alone are the true Bhagavan, the blessed, the essence of all laws, the image of all wisdom of the whole present world. You bear all things. (T-61b, from Kleuker's version of a Brahman source)

> God is immaterial, therefore he is above all conception; since he is invisible, he can have no shape. But from what we can confirm from his works, we can conclude that he is eternal, omnipotent, omniscient, omnipresent. (T-93b, Georg Forster's version of a Brahman source, with Beethoven's underlining)

Thus Beethoven perceived God as transcendent and unsearchable; yet he also perceived a loving God who was immanent in the world and nature, and could respond to prayer. Like the Heiligenstadt Testament, the Tagebuch in places takes the form of a prayer addressed directly to God:

> O God, God, look down on the unhappy B[eethoven], let it not last any longer like this. (T-3)

God, God, my refuge, my rock, O my all, you see my inner being and know how it pains me to have to make someone suffer by my good works for my dear Karl!!! O hear, ever ineffable, hear me, your unhappy unhappiest of all mortals. (T-160)

Sacrifice yet again all trivialities of social life to your art, O God above all. (T-169)

From his religious beliefs sprang Beethoven's attitudes to life in general, and this idea of self-sacrifice is a recurrent theme in his life and writings, appearing several other times in the Tagebuch:

Submission, inmost submission to your fate, only this can give you the sacrifices ... for the business of service. (T-1)

I must not continue my present everyday life; art also demands this sacrifice. (T-25)

Let everything that is called life be sacrificed to the sublime and a sanctuary of art; let me live, even if it be with assistance if it can be found. (T-40)

You shall dispense deeds, not questions; sacrifice yourself without fame and reward! First practise wonders, if you wish to reveal them; only thus can you fulfil your being. (T-60a, taken from Zacharias Werner, *Die Söhne des Thals*, 1802)

For Beethoven, such sacrifice was necessary in order to accomplish great and lasting deeds, and his lofty ambitions are frequently evident in the Tagebuch.

To my most sublime thoughts lend elevation, add to them truths that last for ever. (T-17)

Let me not sink into the dust without deeds or fame. No, first complete something great, of which future generations too shall hear. (T-49, from *The Iliad*)

Let the motive be in the deed and not in the outcome. Be not one whose motive for action is the hope of reward. Let not your life go by in inactivity. Be industrious, fulfil your duty, banish all thought of the result and the outcome, whether it be good or bad. (T-64b, from the *Bhagavad-Gita*)

Brave and excellent people lead to noble and praiseworthy deeds … (T-68a)

What greater thing can be given to a man than fame and praise and immortality? (T-114, from Pliny)

Sertorius did not mind the <u>appearance of dishonour that was present, and considered he was simply buying time, which is the most valuable thing for a man who wishes to accomplish important things</u>. (T-150, from Plutarch, with Beethoven's underlining)

But he who thinks nobly and executes noble actions, his worthy fame is spread widely by strangers, among the peoples on earth, and everyone blesses the good man. (T-170, from *The Odyssey*)

Beethoven's eagerness to embrace such attitudes lies at the heart of his composing. He did not compose for immediate gain or reward ('banish all thought of the result and the outcome'), but to 'complete something great, of which future generations … shall hear', so as to achieve 'immortality' in the classical sense of an immortal name. He sought elevation even for his 'most sublime thoughts' by incessant refinement of his ideas through his sketching, so that his fame would 'spread widely' and everyone would bless him. And to achieve this, time was his most important resource, which meant that he was always extremely industrious. Even rest was part of his mission:

Rest in diversion in order to act all the more forcefully in art. (T-25)

To achieve his aims required not only sacrifices but also endurance and patience, as he had already indicated in the Heiligenstadt Testament. He therefore urged himself on through a number of Tagebuch entries that encourage persistence and endurance in the face of misfortune:

The best way not to think of your misfortune is through activity. (T-7a)

For Fate gave people the courage to endure. (T-26, from *The Iliad*)

Show your power, Fate! We are not masters of ourselves; what is decided must be, and so be it! (T-73)

The main indication of a distinguished man: steadfastness in adverse and harsh circumstances. (T-93a)

(Really, in truth) a droplet hollows out a stone. (T-125a, from Ovid; the parentheses are Beethoven's)

Beethoven showed much interest in the Homeric concept of Fate, either as inexorable, as in the third of the above quotations, or as something that one can to some extent resist and determine by one's actions. The Ovid quotation is obviously intended metaphorically as persistence triumphing over obduracy.

He also found spiritual support from the example of earlier great composers, as is clear from the following entry:

Portraits of Handel, Bach, Gluck, Mozart, and Haydn in my room ... They can help me lay claim to endurance. (T-43)

The five composers named were evidently those he regarded most highly at that time. Several reports indicate that he admired Handel above all others, followed by Mozart. He also recognized the genius of Bach, and had dedicated a set of sonatas to his former teacher Haydn. Gluck is rarely mentioned, but Beethoven had encountered some of his operas and clearly valued them. Another composer mentioned positively elsewhere in the Tagebuch is C. P. E. Bach, whose music Beethoven regarded as well worth studying. The idea of having portraits of five composers recalls his desire to retain a portrait of his grandfather, which had been in the possession of his family in Bonn. He did not initially bring it to Vienna with him in 1792 but later made a special request for it to be sent to him there, and he preserved it carefully thereafter.

The inspiration of great composers, together with Beethoven's own desire to 'complete something great' for future generations, led to plans for ambitious compositions, which he was contemplating even during his fallow periods of 1813 and 1817. The Tagebuch reveals several such ideas. In summer 1813 he was contemplating a setting of Adolf Müllner's play *Die Schuld*, and copied down several passages from it as well as noting some plans for setting it to music (T-7b–9), although no music sketches are known for this work. It was in 1816–17, however, that he began to note down ambitions to compose something grander and more glorious than ever before, as is evident from several Tagebuch entries.

> Leave aside operas and everything, and write only for your own manner – and then a cowl where you end this unhappy life. (T-84)

> Finish the sonata and the trio. (T-91)

> The concert should consist of two parts, the first part a new symphony and the second part a cantata. (T-98)

> Something must happen – either a journey and for this write the necessary works or an opera ... (T-116)

> There is no other way of saving yourself except [to go] from here, only through this can you again lift yourself to the heights of your art, whereas here you sink in the commonplace. Only a symphony ... and then away, away, away ... (T-119)

Thus by 1816 Beethoven had grown tired of staying in a rut and composing just another commonplace sonata or concerto, where the result would not be qualitatively or stylistically different from his previous achievements. He had to urge himself to finish a sonata (Op. 101) and a trio that he had begun, and he never did complete the trio, an interesting though not outstandingly innovative piano trio in F minor, of which most of the exposition survives in a somewhat sketchy form,[2] rather like the opening of the unfinished piano concerto of the previous year. Yet while composing very little and jotting down a diversity of unfulfilled fragments (notably in his Scheide Sketchbook of 1815–16), he began harbouring ideas of something far more elevated and uplifting. An opera or a symphony had been considered, while the notion of a grand choral cantata was beginning to take shape, and was developed in some entries of 1818:

---

[2] See Nicholas Marston, 'In the "Twilight Zone": Beethoven's Unfinished Piano Trio in F minor', *Journal of the Royal Musical Association*, 131 (2006), pp. 227–86.

Write a national song on the Leipzig October and perform this every year. N.B. each nation with its own march and the *Te Deum laudamus*. (T-153)

[missing word] written in which a melodrama also appears, in short a cantata with chorus ... a stage work so that one can show oneself in everything ... (T-162)

In order to write true church music go through all the ecclesiastical chants of the monks etc. Also look there for the verses in the most correct translations and most perfect prosody of all Christian-Catholic psalms and hymns in general. (T-168)

The plan for a national song to commemorate the Battle of Leipzig of October 1813, which could have become a second and more grandiose battle composition to follow *Wellingtons Sieg*, soon evaporated; but Beethoven shortly afterwards considered incorporating the German form of the *Te Deum* (a famous Latin hymn by St Ambrose, 'We praise thee O God') into the finale of the second of the two symphonies he was planning to compose for London. This was his earliest idea for a choral finale for a symphony, an idea that eventually emerged in the Ninth Symphony with his setting of Schiller's *An die Freude*. We also see in these Tagebuch entries an inkling of what was to become his *Missa solemnis*. Beethoven was now giving increasing attention to religion, as the rationalism of the eighteenth-century Enlightenment gave way to new modes of thought in the nineteenth century, and he was seeking for the first time to find a way of writing 'true church music', recognizing that most of the church music by his contemporaries was far removed from the purity of plainchant.

The Tagebuch entry that perhaps best embraces the heart of all the above ideas is part of another quotation from Werner's *Die Söhne des Thals*:

Be more than your fate, love the hater, and seek the great good of self-completion in creating. You are the mirror image of the Eternal. When people curse Him, He smiles, and creates paradise around their huts. (T-60d)

Here are the goodness and greatness of God, the lofty ambition of creating, the struggle with Fate, and the desire to do good in the world. These are all concepts that underpin Beethoven's entire life and output.

Further insights into his beliefs and attitudes can naturally be found elsewhere. His letters provide many examples, while his contemporaries left numerous reminiscences about him. These extend and amplify our knowledge of Beethoven's outlook but do not fundamentally alter it.[3] The Tagebuch, being a private document intended for nobody but himself, betrays his true motivations far better than any public statement or personal communication, which may have some unstated ulterior motive. It confirms the impression conveyed in other sources that Beethoven was motivated throughout his life by goodness and kindness, and the desire to accomplish great things for the benefit of mankind. One can see why Antonie Brentano described him once as 'even greater as a human being than as an artist',[4] a view shared by several other acquaintances of Beethoven's.

---

[3] For a fuller account, see, for example, Barry Cooper, 'Beethoven's Beliefs and Opinions', in Cooper (ed.), *The Beethoven Compendium*, pp. 142–60. Another angle on Beethoven's thought can be found in Glenn Stanley, 'Beethoven at Work: Musical Activist and Thinker', in Glenn Stanley (ed.), *The Cambridge Companion to Beethoven*, (Cambridge: Cambridge University Press, 2000), pp. 14–31.
[4] BB-1289.

FIVE

LATE BEETHOVEN (1818–1827)

A very grand sonata

Towards the end of 1817 Beethoven began to recover sufficient energy to resume composing at something approaching his normal rate. He did not, however, resume and complete the unfinished piano concerto and unfinished piano trio that he had been working on earlier. During his unproductive months he had been rethinking the nature of his art, and he was determined to raise his music to still more elevated levels than before, as he hinted in several comments in his Tagebuch (see 'Beethoven's beliefs and attitudes: the Tagebuch', pp. 107–114). The Ninth Symphony had now been begun and was to become far longer and more complex than any previous symphony, although there is little evidence of this in the early sketches apart from his plan for a choral finale in a symphony, accompanied by a tenfold(!) increase in the strings. Meanwhile he also embarked on a new and unprecedentedly grandiose and complex piano sonata, intended from the start to be dedicated to his friend and pupil Archduke Rudolph. This was the so-called 'Hammerklavier' Sonata in B flat, Op. 106. Since the end of the Napoleonic wars Beethoven had been trying to introduce German terms where possible, in place of Italian ones, and he tried to find the best German word for 'pianoforte'. After some discussion the word 'Hammerklavier' was decided on, and was already used for his previous sonata, Op. 101, before reappearing for Op. 106. The pounding hammer-blows at the start of the latter, however, have meant that the word (which was also used in the autograph of Beethoven's next sonata, Op. 109) has become applied almost exclusively to this sonata. The first two movements were written for Rudolph's name-day, 17 April 1818, and the remaining two movements were written later that year. It was labelled a 'Grand Sonata', a term reserved for sonatas of unusual difficulty and length that would challenge both listener and performer; but the massive 'Hammerklavier' raises the concept of the 'grand sonata' to a totally new level, especially in its extraordinarily powerful but intricate fugal finale.

One factor that may have encouraged Beethoven to write a new piano sonata was the prospect of receiving a new piano. In 1803 he had been sent a piano by the Parisian firm Erard, in recognition of his outstanding achievements, and he had responded shortly thereafter by writing the 'Waldstein' Sonata, which was at the time the grandest of his grand sonatas. Now his extraordinary reputation induced the London firm of Broadwood & Sons to send him one of their latest models, which was despatched in January 1818. It still survives in the Hungarian National Museum, Budapest, and bears the signatures of five of the leading London musicians of the time. Beethoven wrote to thank Thomas Broadwood on 3 February, although the instrument was held up and did not actually reach him until late spring, by which time much of the 'Hammerklavier' Sonata had been completed. It is perhaps significant that, although the sonata as a whole uses every single note of an expanded compass of six and a half octaves, which was available on newer Viennese pianos, the last two movements keep to the six-octave range of the Broadwood instrument.

20. *Beethoven's Erard piano, which he received as a gift from the Paris firm in 1803.*

Caring for Karl

In late January 1818 Beethoven's nephew finally left Giannatasio's boarding school and came to live with him, taught by a personal tutor and studying music with Beethoven for two and a half hours daily. It cannot have been an easy time for either of them, for Beethoven was not accustomed to having an 11-year-old in his lodgings and was evidently not an ideal parent: he was full of demands and rather overbearing, expecting levels of industry comparable to his own. One of the biggest problems, however, was Beethoven's deafness, for Karl needed a companion to talk to and this was almost impossible with Beethoven. It was probably about this time that Beethoven found it necessary to resort to having his visitors write down their side of conversations on scraps of paper or little notebooks. Although one or two such fragments of conversation may date from 1817, the earliest surviving conversation book was used in February–March 1818. There may have been some earlier ones, and since the second surviving one dates from March–May 1819 several are probably lost from the intervening period. It is in fact remarkable that these early ones have survived at all, given their ephemeral nature. Beethoven may have preserved the first one because he had entered some musical ideas (mainly scales based in the old church modes), which he may have considered useful for possible reference in a composition or for instructing Karl.

About 139 conversation books survive altogether from the period 1818–27,[1] and they provide incredibly detailed insights into Beethoven's everyday existence, even though they normally give only one side of the conversation since he replied orally except on rare occasions when he wanted to avoid being overheard. He did, however, make plenty of entries in the notebooks, such as shopping lists, memoranda, music sketches, and copies of newspaper advertisements. Though the books were used mainly at home, he sometimes took one to a restaurant if he was having a meal with friends, as is clear from several groups of entries. The very first entry in the first book, which is by Beethoven himself, mentions Karl, and one of the next entries is in Karl's hand. It concerns some sausage: 'The skin without sausage is also good, but with sausage it is better than the meat alone.' Such totally mundane entries are interspersed with occasional references to productions at the theatre, news matters, and sometimes discussions related to music, including performances of Beethoven's works. On their own they are tantalizingly elusive and difficult to interpret because of their one-sided nature and often obscure references, but they have become much better understood through detailed research of their context.

---

[1] They are transcribed in Karl-Heinz Köhler and others (eds.), *Ludwig van Beethovens Konversationshefte* (abbreviated here to BKh), 11 vols to date (Leipzig: Deutscher Verlag für Musik, 1968–2001). The editors provide extensive notes illuminating many aspects of the conversations.

In addition to the conversation books, many conversations with Beethoven were written on slates and then erased, while on better days people could sometimes make themselves understood by shouting into his ear, perhaps aided by an ear-trumpet. Thus there would be numerous gaps in the conversation record even if all the books had survived, and evidence suggests that several are missing; there are none from 1821, for example, although Beethoven was ill for much of that year and would have had relatively few conversations.

During 1818 Johanna was rarely able to see Karl, and usually only through subterfuge, since Beethoven considered her to be such a bad influence on the boy that he felt it better that she be kept away as much as reasonable. She eventually petitioned the court, known as the *Landrecht*, that she might have more access and control and perhaps become co-guardian. Her petition was rejected in September, as was a second petition the following month. In early December, however, Karl ran away to her, causing Beethoven great distress and prompting Johanna to make a third petition. This was heard on 11 December, with Karl, Beethoven, and Johanna all interviewed. During the hearing, Beethoven was asked about his plans for Karl, and he stated that if he were of noble birth he would in due course send the boy to a school for noble children (the Theresianum). This was an unfortunate admission, since the *Landrecht* was the court for nobles; they had assumed that the 'van' in Beethoven's name was equivalent to 'von' in Austria, where this prefix indicated nobility, but Beethoven stated that this was not the case with the Dutch prefix 'van', and that he had no proof of nobility. He believed that his widely recognized achievements, his connections with the aristocracy, and his moral rectitude entitled him to be counted as a nobleman, but the *Landrecht* did not accept this and transferred his case to a lower court, the Viennese *Magistrat*. Beethoven was mortified, regarding this court as suitable only for 'inn-keepers, cobblers, and tailors'.[2] The *Magistrat* duly sided with Johanna, showing conspicuous partiality in her favour. The decision on 11 January 1819 is not recorded explicitly, but the *Magistrat* assumed for themselves a supervisory role as a kind of panel of 'over-guardians' (*Obervormundschaft*) and asked Beethoven to nominate a new guardian in place of himself. Beethoven nominated Matthias von Tuscher, who was appointed on 26 March but resigned on 5 July.

Meanwhile Beethoven had continued to function as guardian in practice, and arranged for Karl to be placed in an educational institute run by Johann Kudlich, with a private tutor, and then on 22 June in an institute run by Joseph Blöchlinger. In September, however, the *Magistrat* accepted Tuscher's resignation but appointed Johanna, not Beethoven, as guardian, along with Leopold Nussböck. The following month, after returning from

---

[2] A-979; BB-1348.

his customary summer break outside the city, Beethoven asked the *Magistrat* to return the guardianship to him, but his pleas were twice rejected, and he was forced to turn to the Appeal Court. He wrote to them in January 1820, and then drafted an enormous document the following month, in which he put down all the details of the entire history of the case as seen from his point of view (see 'Beethoven and his nephew: the appeal memorandum', pp. 137–147, for an extended account of this famous document). Eventually the Appeal Court decided in his favour, and he was granted guardianship along with a co-guardian (Karl Peters), which the court deemed necessary on account of Beethoven's deafness. The decision was announced on 8 April 1820, and Beethoven was ecstatic at the outcome. Karl was saved from the woman whom Beethoven had once dubbed 'the Queen of the Night' (after the evil character in *Die Zauberflöte*), a woman who several of Beethoven's companions agreed should be entirely removed from influencing Karl.[3] Even the *Magistrat* had accepted 'the necessity of withdrawing the boy from the mother's influence',[4] and she was actually pregnant during the Appeal Court hearing, giving birth to an illegitimate daughter Ludovika in June 1820. Some may question the wisdom of the court's decision, since it was not a perfect solution and seemed hard on Johanna; but Beethoven's conviction that it was in Karl's best interests is undeniable, and the boy did ultimately fulfil some of Beethoven's hopes by turning out a fine and prosperous citizen (married with five children), despite many problems along the way.

Beethoven's 'greatest work'

Throughout the final year of the guardianship dispute, Beethoven was working on his *Missa solemnis* or Mass in D, which he repeatedly described as his 'greatest work', even after the completion of his Ninth Symphony.[5] The idea for its composition came from Archduke Rudolph, who had for several years been in line for succession as Archbishop of Olmütz (now Olomouc). The previous archbishop finally died on 20 January 1819, and Rudolph informed Beethoven of his own forthcoming succession to the post in a message written in late February. The message does not survive, but Beethoven's reply of 3 March makes clear that Rudolph's message had asked him to compose a grand mass for the installation ceremony the following year, for after sending his congratulations to Rudolph he adds almost as an afterthought: 'The day on which a High Mass composed by me shall be performed at the ceremonies for Your Imperial Highness will be the finest day of my life.'[6] This could only have been stated in response to a request from Rudolph.

---

[3] See Cooper, *Beethoven*, pp. 274–5 (2nd edn, p. 296).
[4] TF, p. 724.
[5] See e.g. A-1079, 1269; BB-1468, 1788.
[6] A-948 (misdated June 1819); BB-1292.

21. Portrait of Beethoven by Joseph Stieler, about April 1820, showing him composing the Credo of the Missa solemnis. *The features are a good likeness of the composer, but the manuscript is far from accurate.*

From the outset this was to be no ordinary work, and Beethoven made thorough preparations for it. He probably went through some volumes of plainchant, as in the plan noted the previous year in his Tagebuch, for certain parts of the *Missa solemnis*, notably the passage 'et incarnatus est', create a modal effect that recalls that of chant; and about that time he made a setting of an actual chant, 'Pange lingua'. He also made a detailed study of the text of the Mass, writing out an annotated translation and ensuring he understood theological subtleties such as the difference between being 'born' and being 'incarnate'.[7]

Beethoven still had nearly a year ahead of him for completion of the work, and took time off during April to May to draft a large-scale set of piano variations before beginning detailed work on the mass. These variations were the famous Diabelli Variations. The publisher and composer Anton Diabelli had conceived the idea of creating a monument

---

[7] See William Drabkin, *Beethoven: Missa solemnis* (Cambridge: Cambridge University Press, 1991), pp. 14–15.

to Viennese music by composing a waltz and asking every resident composer to write a variation on it. The first invitations were probably sent out in April, but Beethoven had no interest in contributing a mere single variation to such a project (although Archduke Rudolph did, along with forty-nine other composers including Schubert, Hummel, Moscheles, Czerny, Liszt, and many minor figures). Beethoven was equally reluctant to write just a small batch of variations, for he had just completed sixteen such sets for George Thomson (Opp. 105 and 107). Thus he conceived the idea of writing a huge set, comparable to Bach's 'Goldberg' Variations, which he seems to have known at least by reputation. The idea may also have been sparked off by a massive set of forty variations that Rudolph had recently completed on a theme by Beethoven. Beethoven had described Rudolph's set as masterly, although he proposed certain improvements that Rudolph willingly adopted. Variations were a genre that could be written quite quickly (as Beethoven had shown in his sixteen sets for Thomson), and he had soon drafted an incomplete set of twenty-three variations on Diabelli's theme. He then laid these aside (eventually resuming and completing the work nearly four years later), and returned to the *Missa solemnis* for detailed sketching during the rest of 1819.

Rudolph's installation ceremony was fixed for 9 March 1820, and Beethoven continued to expect his mass to be ready for the occasion until early February. His enormous efforts to separate his nephew from the influence of Johanna, however, occupied far more of his time than anticipated, and he had reached only the middle of the Credo, the third of the five movements of the mass, when he had to turn his attention to the memorandum he was preparing for the Appeal Court hearing. This exhausting task left him almost no time to work on the mass, and the ceremony at Olmütz finally went ahead without the new work. Thereafter its composition proceeded more slowly and intermittently as he turned his attention to other works, notably a revision of some folksong settings (Op. 108) and his last three piano sonatas (Opp. 109–11). A trial performance of the Kyrie and Gloria of the mass appears to have taken place on 25 October 1821,[8] but Rudolph did not receive his presentation copy of the complete work until March 1823, and it did not appear in print until 1827.

What Rudolph received was a work of extreme sophistication, where the music operates on several levels at once, ranging from almost absurd directness of expression (such as huge downward leaps to illustrate the word 'descendit') to amazing technical complexity in the fugue for the words 'et vitam venturi saeculi' ('and the life of the world to come'). Yet the whole work reveals the deepest profundity of musical and theological insight, combined with intense emotion. The score is headed, 'From the

---

[8] See David Wyn Jones, 'The *Missa solemnis* Premiere: First Rites', *The Musical Times*, 139 (Autumn 1998), pp. 25–8.

heart – May it return – To the heart!' Beethoven wrote on 16 September 1824: 'My chief aim was to awaken and permanently instil religious feelings as much in the singers as in the listeners.'[9] He was surely right to describe the *Missa solemnis* as his greatest work.

Financial problems

While the mass was still unfinished, in early 1821, Beethoven fell ill, and he completed virtually nothing for almost a year. When a friend apparently asked him in November that year to send anything he had composed since February, Beethoven responded by sending a single fourteen-bar canon, and indicated he had written nothing else.[10] This lack of productivity seriously affected his financial circumstances, for he was still providing most of the funds for Karl's education, while his annuity was barely adequate for his own needs. Although he had substantial funds in the form of bank shares, these had been set aside as a legacy for Karl (as he indicated in his memorandum for the Appeal Court) and therefore could not be touched. Thus he urgently needed some immediate income. Yet he had begun three huge works that were still far from finished – the *Missa solemnis*, the Diabelli Variations, and the Ninth Symphony – and completing any of these would take some time. He wrote to Franz Brentano on 12 November informing him that the mass was still not quite ready since it needed checking (a comment that implies it was by then complete, which it may well have been, although he made many further additions and revisions thereafter). He then added that 'in view of my basic needs I had to finish off several pot-boilers',[11] which delayed completion of the mass. Yet the only two works he was writing in late 1821 apart from the mass were his last two piano sonatas, Opp. 110 and 111. It is quite amazing that he was able to deride two of the greatest sonatas in the piano literature as mere 'pot-boilers' (*Brot-Arbeiten*), and it is an indication of the extraordinary elevation of his even greater works of this period.

The two sonatas were finally completed by early 1822, but their sale to the publisher Adolf Schlesinger still did not bring in sufficient income for Karl's needs. Several publishers, notably Carl Friedrich Peters of Leipzig, had written to him asking what works they could buy, but he had nothing new to offer them apart from the mass and the Diabelli Variations, neither of which was ready. He offered the mass to several publishers at this stage, but did not actually send it to any of them. Instead he began rounding up as many old but unpublished works as he could find. He then drew up a price list of those he could make available and sent the information to Peters, hoping that he could quickly gain some much-needed income that

---

[9] A-1307; BB-1875.
[10] See Cooper, *Beethoven*, p. 284 (2nd edn, p. 306).
[11] A-1059; BB-1445.

way. The list even included works not begun: piano sonatas and string quartets that Peters could have 'quite soon'. Peters agreed to take a quartet and several of the existing works, including a set of bagatelles; but these needed more attention before they were ready, and when Beethoven did finally send six bagatelles (Op. 119 Nos 1–6), some military marches, and three songs in early 1823, Peters perceptively observed that some of them looked rather dated, and he made excuses not to publish any of them. Thus the greatest composer of the day, who had frequently been criticized for writing music that was too long and too difficult, found that composing short, easy piano pieces would not always guarantee a sale, although the bagatelles and songs were eventually taken by other publishers.

Meanwhile in November 1822 Beethoven had received two requests that were to result in work that he surely found far more rewarding and elevating: one for a symphony and one for some quartets. At this stage of his life he wanted to write only the most elevated types of music, and longed to avoid the need to write more 'pot-boilers'. Thus he wrote to Ferdinand Ries in July 1822 asking how much the Philharmonic Society of London could offer for a symphony (the plan for an actual visit to London, with two symphonies, had been watered down somewhat). The November reply indicated a figure of £50 – approximately 500 silver florins – which would be enough to cover Karl's costs for over half a year. Thus Beethoven resumed work on his Ninth Symphony about that time, and also jotted down some brief ideas for a Tenth Symphony. The other request for new works came out of the blue from the Russian Prince Galitzin in St Petersburg, who asked Beethoven to write one, two, or three new quartets and to name his price. Beethoven replied proposing 50 ducats, equivalent to 225 silver florins (another three months or more of Karl's costs), for each of three quartets, and Galitzin readily agreed.

Beethoven was now promising rather more than he could easily deliver. So many publishers were wanting his mass that he proposed writing two or even three to satisfy demand. The Philharmonic Society was expecting the Ninth Symphony. The local music society, the Gesellschaft der Musikfreunde, had commissioned (and paid for) an oratorio. Diabelli was becoming impatient for the set of variations that Beethoven had promised nearly four years earlier. And Peters was still expecting a string quartet, as now was Galitzin. Thus when Beethoven wrote to Galitzin on 23 January 1823 promising the first new quartet at the end of February 'or mid-March at the latest', he perhaps wisely omitted to indicate which year. In the end it was sent to the prince two years later, in March 1825, with the other two quartets following later still.

Ninth Symphony

After dealing with the odds and ends sent to Peters in February 1823, Beethoven concentrated on the Diabelli Variations. He cancelled one of the twenty-three variations from his 1819 draft, but added eleven new ones plus a coda to make a huge work that lasts about an hour in performance. It covers the whole gamut of human emotion, and develops the process of variation technique in extraordinary new ways. When it was published it was announced as no ordinary set of variations but 'a great and important masterpiece … such as only Beethoven could deliver', and worthy of a place beside Bach's masterpiece (the 'Goldberg' Variations).

Immediately this work was finished, Beethoven began intensive sketching for the Ninth Symphony, as usual taking each movement in turn. By this time he had decided on the standard four-movement plan, but with a chorus and solo voices joining in for the finale, singing excerpts of Schiller's *An die Freude*, which he had been wanting to set to music ever since the 1790s. The idea of introducing voices in a regular symphony was unprecedented, and seemed almost a contradiction, since a symphony at that time was by definition an instrumental work, or occasionally an instrumental section in a larger vocal work such as an opera. The idea also posed fresh challenges, since it was going to be difficult to make the finale seem to belong with the rest of the work; but in the end Beethoven solved this problem triumphantly by several means, which included introducing brief references to each of the first three movements near the start of the finale. Almost throughout the time he was working intensively on the symphony, however, he was troubled by a serious and painful eye infection, which made him susceptible to bright lights and for a short while prevented him from working altogether. The illness has not been diagnosed with certainty, but it seems most likely to have been uveitis.[12]

By the end of the year the illness had still not fully cleared up, and the symphony was still not ready, although Beethoven had promised Ries as early as April that it would be sent soon. The finale became a huge cantata-like movement in many sections, based around an extraordinarily simple, folk-like tune worked into a highly elaborate structure that can be viewed in any of several ways and has caused endless debate among analysts. The symphony was finally completed early in 1824, although a copy did not reach London until nearly the end of the year. The agreement with the Philharmonic Society stipulated merely that the society would receive a new symphony in manuscript, with the provision that it must not be published for at least eighteen months thereafter (a provision that Beethoven duly respected); but there was no restriction on performing the work in Vienna, and plans were soon being made for such a performance to take place. Beethoven was unconvinced, however, that the new work would be well received in Vienna, where Rossini's music had recently

---

[12] See Peter J. Davies, *Beethoven in Person: His Illnesses, Deafness, and Death* (Westport, CT: Greenwood, 2001), pp. 201–5; François Martin Mai, *Diagnosing Genius: The Life and Death of Beethoven* (Montreal: McGill-Queen's University Press, 2007), pp. 166–8. Both authors consider other possible diagnoses.

become extremely popular, almost to the exclusion of more serious art, and he considered arranging the premiere for Berlin. He was persuaded not to by some of his chief admirers in Vienna, who even went to the trouble of presenting him with a petition in February signed by thirty people. They urged him to present his latest works, namely the *Missa solemnis* and the Ninth Symphony, in Vienna at a specially arranged concert, and he agreed to do so.

Information about preparations for the concert can be found in great detail in Beethoven's correspondence and especially his conversation books, though not everything is covered. For the programme, it was decided to include three movements from the *Missa solemnis* – the Kyrie, Credo, and Agnus Dei – but they had to be advertised as 'grand hymns' to circumvent the ban on performing church music in the theatre. The Ninth Symphony was put last on the programme to provide a fitting climax, and the first item was the overture *Die Weihe des Hauses* (The Consecration of the House), which Beethoven had composed in 1822 for an adaptation of *Die Ruinen von Athen* to open a new theatre in the Viennese suburbs. At one stage the concert was being planned for late March, then 7 April, but eventually it was fixed for 7 May 1824. Several venues were considered, since each had its own drawbacks and Beethoven had used a variety of locations for his earlier concerts. Eventually the Kärntnerthortheater, scene of the premiere of the 1814 version of *Fidelio*, was chosen. One advantage was that the theatre had its own resident chorus and orchestra, which could be engaged, along with lighting and the theatre itself, for 400 florins. The chorus there consisted of thirty-two boys (sixteen treble and sixteen alto) supported by thirty-four men on the lower parts,[13] but this was felt to be insufficient for Beethoven's concert, and so it was strengthened on 7 May by amateurs from the Gesellschaft der Musikfreunde, which included women and girls for the upper voices. Altogether there were probably well over a hundred singers taking part.

Everything was arranged very much at the last minute. The theatre chorus director, Ignaz Dirzka, did not receive the chorus parts until 26 or 27 April, and held the first choral rehearsal on the 28th,[14] while the tenor soloist, Anton Haitzinger, had to await his part until 2 May. The two female soloists were both very young – the soprano, Henriette Sontag, only 18 and the contralto, Caroline Unger, 20 – and still did not know their parts five days before the performance. The bass part was given to Joseph Preisinger, but he had to be replaced by Joseph Seipelt about two days before the concert. There were two full rehearsals, which were as many as might be expected – often there was only one for a large concert – and some sectional rehearsals.

---

[13] BKh, vol. 6, p. 63.
[14] BKh, vol. 6, pp. 72 and 102.

The minimal rehearsal time must have limited the standard achievable, but the performance was highly successful. Beethoven was nominally conductor, in that he set the speeds for each movement, but the main direction was entrusted to Michael Umlauf, assisted by the leader, Ignaz Schuppanzigh. The theatre was packed (apart from the imperial box), and the audience gave rapturous applause. At one point, probably after the second movement of the symphony, Unger had to tug at Beethoven's sleeve to enable him to acknowledge the applause, since he was too deaf to hear it and had been turning over pages with his back to the audience. The enthusiasm was no doubt as much for the efforts of the performers, and for the fact that Beethoven had finally put on a concert, as for the quality of the music. Nevertheless, many sensed that this was an extraordinary occasion, and that the music marked a major advance on anything previously composed, whether by Beethoven or anyone else. A second performance took place on 23 May, though for various reasons this attracted a much smaller audience and less enthusiasm, and Beethoven never again put on a concert, though he occasionally thought about doing so.

The late quartets

Soon after the second performance of the Ninth Symphony, Beethoven was at last able to turn to the three string quartets that he had promised to Prince Galitzin, and he worked hard at them for about the next eighteen months, though illness caused a few interruptions. As mentioned earlier (see pp. 27–8), much of the preparatory work for these quartets took the form of score sketches, in which rough drafts were written out on four separate staves, one for each instrument. Often in a particular bar Beethoven filled in details for only one or two of the instruments, but in many places where each had important and contrasting material all four were sketched. Beethoven had occasionally sketched in this format before, but now it became a regular and integral part of his composing method. This enabled him to compose quartets of unprecedented complexity, involving a new kind of part-writing, as he himself observed. All four instruments were given parts that were highly individual, yet they still blended together into a homogeneous whole. He also considered new structures in place of the traditional four-movement format. One early sketch for the first Galitzin quartet (in E flat major) suggests a six-movement plan, although in the end Beethoven restricted himself to the normal four movements. For the next two quartets (A minor and B flat major), however, he wrote five and six movements respectively, and the A minor quartet has before the finale an additional section that could be counted as another short movement.

Hand in hand with the composition of these three quartets went plans to sell them to publishers. Beethoven was still very short of funds for Karl, for his two grand concerts had brought him far less than he was expecting, owing largely to the huge costs of copying the extra parts for the voices as well as for the orchestra. Thus he was very happy to find that publishers were queuing up to buy his next quartet. The first was sold to Schott's of Mainz for 50 ducats (225 silver florins), but thereafter he was able to raise the price to 80 ducats per quartet and still find plenty of willing purchasers in the publishing world. The second quartet eventually went to Moritz Schlesinger of Paris (whose father Adolf had commissioned Beethoven's last three piano sonatas); and the third went to Mathias Artaria, a member of the Artaria publishing family in Vienna but running an independent firm. Since some firms were quicker than others in publication, however, the opus numbers are out of sequence; thus the three quartets have the opus numbers 127, 132, and 130 respectively (Opp. 128 and 129 are lesser works, while Op. 131, the C sharp minor quartet, was written after all three of these).

While composing the second quartet, Beethoven suffered a serious illness in April 1825 and had to stay in bed with an intestinal inflammation. He was visited on 18 April by Dr Anton Braunhofer, who was not his usual doctor but had previously treated Karl. Braunhofer prescribed a strict diet, which he indicated in Beethoven's conversation book: 'Morning: chocolate drink but without vanilla, with milk or water. Lunchtime: soup according to my instructions. Soft-boiled eggs without pepper.' The instructions for the soup were then written down for Beethoven by his nephew: 'Your soup must be made for you without parsley but with barley, and if you have the appetite, a couple of soft-boiled eggs. Otherwise you mustn't eat anything.' Coffee, wine, and spices were specifically forbidden.[15] The diet was a success and Beethoven soon recovered, as the doctor had predicted. Beethoven's response was extraordinary: for the very next movement of the quartet he was writing, he composed what he entitled 'Heiliger Dankgesang eines Genesenen an die Gottheit, in der Lydischen Tonart' (Sacred song of thanks from a convalescent to the Godhead, in the Lydian Mode). It is a most unusual movement, alternating a solemn chorale with sections marked 'feeling new strength'; and the Lydian Mode, F major but with B naturals, gives a timeless, exalted character. Rarely has a composer responded so immediately, and with such effect, to an event in his personal life.

By now Beethoven was attracting visitors from far and wide, all eager to make or renew their acquaintance with him. These included the London-based Johann Reinhold Schultz and the composer Carl Maria von Weber in autumn 1823; the Berlin poet Ludwig Rellstab in spring 1824; the London harp maker Johann Andreas Stumpff a few months later; the Dutchman Samson Moses de Boer in August 1825; the Danish composer Johann Kuhlau a month later; the Paris-based publisher Moritz Schlesinger

---

[15] BKh, vol. 7, p. 222.

22. *A page (folio 15v) from Beethoven's conversation book no. 83 (no. 87 in BKh), from Monday 18 April 1825. At the top Karl writes 'snow', followed by some comments on making good soup. He then mentions Dr Braunhofer, whose hand appears beneath, asking Beethoven in detail about his symptoms.*

days later; and the English conductor Sir George Smart a few days after that. During most of these visits Beethoven was living at his summer residence in Baden, some miles south of Vienna, and it is noteworthy that so many foreign visitors were prepared to go out of their way to seek him out. Beethoven received all of them cordially, and many of them left enthusiastic accounts of their visits. These accounts are sometimes supplemented by entries in the conversation books, although Schultz made no entries, instead reporting that Beethoven could usually understand if one spoke loudly and slowly. Clearly Beethoven's deafness varied from day to day, and Schultz's visit was on one of the better days.

Kuhlau's visit resulted in a very merry dinner party in Baden, at which Beethoven drank so much champagne that he became uncharacteristically intoxicated and could not remember much afterwards. But he managed to compose a canon on the notes B A C H (German names for B♭ – A – C – B♮), to the words 'Kühl nicht lau' (Cool, not lukewarm, WoO 191), making a clever play of words on Kuhlau's name; Beethoven greatly enjoyed such word-play and puns in general.

Possibly the most significant of the visits he received around that time, however, was Schlesinger's, since it influenced his output of compositions rather more substantially than did Kuhlau's visit. Once the third of the string quartets for Prince Galitzin was nearly finished, Beethoven had to decide what would follow from the long line of possible projects that he had in mind: a Tenth Symphony; an overture on the notes B A C H (a plan that was clearly in the back of his mind as he sketched the Kuhlau canon); an opera entitled *Melusine*, which he had been planning for at least two years with the poet Franz Grillparzer; an oratorio that had been commissioned by the Gesellschaft der Musikfreunde; a second new mass; or another string quartet to appease the publishers who were still clamouring for one. Beethoven actually jotted down a few sketches for the overture and rather more for the symphony, noting in his sketchbook: 'This overture with the new symphony, thus we have a concert at the Kärntnerthor'.[16] The first movement of the symphony was to combine a gentle E flat andante with a stormy allegro in C minor, and a comment beside one of the sketches, 'Come, come, take me away to the transfiguration' (i.e. to heavenly life), implies that these contrasting sections represent heavenly bliss set against earthly struggle. There is also a striking contrast between two main motifs – one rising and one falling – which also seem to evoke a heaven-earth duality. Thus structural and motivic elements in the movement are related to each other in an extraordinary new way, through their poetic implications.[17] Sufficient

---

[16] See Hans-Günter Klein, *Ludwig van Beethoven: Autographe und Abschriften*, Staatsbibliothek Preussischer Kulturbesitz: Kataloge der Musikabteilung, I/2 (Berlin: Merseburger, 1975), p. 22.
[17] See Cooper, *Beethoven*, pp. 336–7 (2nd edn, p. 362).

sketches for the first movement of the symphony survive for it to be possible to produce a performing version purely through development and orchestration of the musical material in the sketches, without the invention of any new thematic ideas. Beethoven recognized in 1825, however, that to complete a large-scale work such as the symphony would take some time, and the opera and oratorio he was envisaging provided the additional problem of obtaining a suitable libretto. String quartets, on the other hand, offered the prospect of more immediate reward, which was still badly needed for Karl's support. What may have finally persuaded Beethoven was a request from Moritz Schlesinger, who wanted three quartets and three quintets. He wrote in the conversation book: 'If you write quartets and quintets you gain for your nephew more money than with any other great works.'[18] Thus Beethoven proceeded to compose two further string quartets (Opp. 131 and 135) and embark on a string quintet, not because he became so absorbed in the medium that he could not bring himself to leave off, as is sometimes claimed, but in direct response to public clamour as filtered through the publishers and especially Schlesinger, who had judged their market carefully. Of the two last quartets, Op. 131 went to Schott's and Op. 135 to Schlesinger, who would gladly have taken as many quartets and quintets as Beethoven was prepared to compose.

The three Galitzin quartets were all given trial performances in Vienna, mostly before small, select groups of listeners. The premiere of Op. 127 on 6 March 1825 was relatively unsuccessful because of its technical difficulties – especially the problem of keeping the four instruments together at the numerous changes of time signature – but subsequent performances were much admired. The work was recognized as so complex, however, that Schott's prepared a score as well as parts, and also a piano duet arrangement, to facilitate study (all Beethoven's previous quartets had been published only as separate instrumental parts).

The finale of Op. 130 in B flat proved even more of a stumbling block for listeners when this quartet was given its premiere on 23 March 1826. Beethoven had contrived to write an enormous and impenetrable fugue, which nobody could fathom after only one hearing (the movement is still a severe challenge for listeners today). It was therefore suggested that the fugue be arranged for piano duet to facilitate study, and the task was entrusted to Anton Halm. Beethoven was dissatisfied with the result, however, and proceeded to make his own piano duet arrangement. Once this had been accepted by Artaria (it eventually appeared as Op. 134), Beethoven decided to publish the string version separately too, as a *Grosse Fuge* (Grand Fugue, Op. 133), and to compose a new finale for Op. 130. According to the usual version of events, it was the publisher who, bearing

---

[18] BKh, vol. 8, p. 102.

in mind the audience reaction to the premiere, asked Beethoven's new young friend Karl Holz to persuade Beethoven to compose a simpler finale, and Beethoven reluctantly agreed so as to earn 15 extra ducats. This narrative seems unlikely, since Beethoven normally rejected any suggestion for modifications to his works, and would not have composed a new finale merely for a few meagre ducats; he could have earned as much writing something else. The narrative is, moreover, confounded by the conversation books. They show that there was no suggestion of a replacement finale until after Beethoven had completed the piano version of the fugue in early September 1826, by which time the string version had been engraved ready for publication as the finale of Op. 130. With the completion of the piano version, however, Beethoven recognized that the fugue had become an independent work, and he decided that the string version also deserved to be published independently. Thus a replacement finale would be needed for Op. 130. This suited Artaria too, since he would effectively obtain a second quartet for only 15 ducats instead of 80.

Another factor that surely helped persuade Beethoven to write a new finale was that he had initially been extremely uncertain how to conclude Op. 130 and had drafted over a dozen possible themes before deciding on the fugue, which exhibits a very different character from any of these earlier themes. It also tends by its size and power to unbalance the rest of the quartet and to overshadow the previous movement, a wonderfully expressive 'Cavatina' whose composition had moved Beethoven himself to tears, and whose main theme had taken nearly a month to compose. Conversely the fugue itself can suffer if heard at the end of a long quartet, for despite its subtle connections to the rest of Op. 130 it actually stands very well on its own, with a structure strikingly similar to that of three of Beethoven's late piano sonatas (Opp. 101, 109, and 110): two movements of limited size and emotional range followed by a much longer and more diverse final movement (though in the *Grosse Fuge* all three 'movements' are linked together). Thus within a week of completing the piano duet version, Beethoven had decided to make the change, and he composed a new finale immediately after finishing Op. 135. The replacement, though not particularly short, is much simpler than the *Grosse Fuge*, and its main theme derives from that of the fourth movement of Op. 130, as the sketches clearly show.[19]

Approaching the end

During the composition of the late quartets, Beethoven's relationship with Karl became increasingly strained. There had been a relatively quiet

---

[19] For a fuller account of the new investigations into the finales of this quartet see Barry Cooper, 'The Two – or Two Dozen – Finales for Beethoven's Quartet Opus 130', *Ad Parnassum*, 8/16 (Oct. 2010), pp. 7–52.

period in the relationship after the court settlement of 1820, but Karl was now approaching manhood and desiring more independence. Beethoven was so concerned for his welfare that he was unwilling to allow this, and tried to keep track of everything Karl did – where he was, the friends he made, and how he spent his money – as well as enlisting his help in some secretarial matters. Karl expressed a wish to join the army, but Beethoven refused to consider this possibility. Instead Karl spent nearly two years at the university (1823–5), studying mainly philosophy and classics, but then transferred to the polytechnic to study business and commerce, timing his transfer to avoid facing examinations. With examinations approaching at the polytechnic in summer 1826, however, Karl felt under enormous pressure from Beethoven, and trapped in a situation beyond what he could cope with. Although he felt confident about the examinations, the strain of the conflict with Beethoven – in many ways a typical conflict between an over-protective parent and an adolescent teenager desperate for more freedom – became too much. He bought two pistols and some bullets on 5 August, and early next morning went out to the beautiful Helenenthal valley just outside Baden, where he and Beethoven had spent many happy times. Like so many people attempting suicide, however, he did not really wish to die; instead he seems to have decided to risk death by shooting very close to, but not at, his head and leaving the outcome to providence. His first shot missed altogether, while the second grazed his temple and left him injured. He was taken first to his mother's and then to the hospital, where he gradually recovered.

Beethoven was absolutely mortified by the event, and it was made worse since Karl obviously could not tell him the true reason for the suicide attempt, and Beethoven was completely incapable of guessing it. When Karl finally made his next entry in a conversation book, it was to reassert his desire to join the army, and Beethoven had to agree. This could not happen immediately, since Karl was too badly injured and needed several months to recover; but there was no return to the polytechnic.

Beethoven's brother Johann proposed that, to aid recuperation, Beethoven and Karl should spend some time at Johann's estate at Gneixendorf, near Krems, two days' journey from Vienna. He had suggested this in the past, but now seemed an opportune time and Beethoven finally agreed. They set out on 28 September, and spent the next two months away from Beethoven's usual haunts. It was to be his last trip away from Vienna. He was already unwell when he left Gneixendorf for the return journey, and became much worse by travelling in an open carriage and spending a night in a freezing inn. On reaching home he went straight to bed and rarely got up thereafter. There was little that doctors could do about his illnesses, which included pneumonia, jaundice, and dropsy, although he underwent four operations to relieve the pressure of water retention caused by the dropsy. Karl finally left for the army on

2 January 1827 after celebrating New Year with Beethoven, and never saw him again. Several gifts arrived. Stumpff, who had gathered from his meeting with Beethoven in 1824 that Handel was his favourite composer, sent a forty-volume edition containing all Handel's major works, and Beethoven was thrilled. When news reached London that he was now too ill to compose, the Philharmonic Society generously sent him £100 – twice what they had paid for the Ninth Symphony – and he was greatly moved by their generosity. In the letter of thanks that he dictated to Schindler, he offered to compose for them 'a new symphony, which lies already sketched in my desk [a clear reference to the unfinished Tenth Symphony], or a new overture'.[20] One final gift, a case of fine Rüdesheim wine sent by Schott's, arrived on 23 or 24 March (there are conflicting reports), but Beethoven's only response was, 'Pity, pity, too late.' These may have been his last words, and he fell into a coma on 24 March. Two days later, about 5.45 p.m. during a violent thunderstorm, a particularly loud clap of thunder caused him to stir for the last time, before he died in the arms of his brother, as Johann himself recorded shortly afterwards.

An autopsy was performed next day, and the original Latin text was rediscovered in 1970, making possible a more reliable translation than that which appeared in older books.[21] It showed that the outer ear was covered by scales of shining skin that hid the eardrum, while the auditory nerves were much shrivelled, especially the left one. The primary cause of death, however, was cirrhosis of the liver. This could have been caused by post-viral hepatitis, but the alcohol that Beethoven had consumed during his lifetime almost certainly played a major part and was probably the main cause.[22] A safe limit for alcohol intake may be no more than four units a day. Beethoven was hardly ever completely intoxicated, but he drank much wine with his meals, and sometimes also spirits or punch. Thus his average intake could have been well over ten units (more than one bottle of wine) per day, which is not particularly excessive but is enough to damage the liver of those who are susceptible, as he evidently was.

By the time of Beethoven's funeral on 29 March, three days after his death, all his hair had been removed by souvenir hunters, and some of it still survives as collectors' items. Recent scientific examination of a few strands of it has indicated that he had raised lead levels, although all other elements tested were normal. It was inevitable that someone of that period would have a higher lead intake than is normal today since lead was so prevalent, in such things as paint and some cooking and eating utensils. However, Beethoven showed no obvious symptoms of lead

---

[20] A-1566; BB-2284. Beethoven's offer was partially fulfilled in 1988 when a completion of the first movement of the symphony, prepared by the present writer and based on these sketches, received its premiere in a concert given by this same society.

[21] See Davies, *Beethoven in Person*, pp. 101–4.

[22] Ibid., *Beethoven in Person*, pp. 177–86; Mai, *Diagnosing Genius*, pp. 141–7.

poisoning, and the precise figures for the lead level in each strand of hair tested (which differed markedly from each other) have not been published. The lead could even have been deposited on the hair externally by some means, perhaps after Beethoven's death. Another study indicates that the lead was not distributed equally along the length of the hair but was concentrated mainly near the scalp. This suggests that most of his lead intake came in the four months before his death, and that he had very little while at Gneixendorf; but this theory has also been challenged, since lead is not deposited in hair in a regular way immediately after intake. Since lead levels in hair are generally regarded as a very unreliable indicator of lead levels in the blood, the extent of any lead poisoning is at present uncertain,[23] and it probably did not contribute to his early death.

Beethoven's funeral procession attracted a huge crowd, estimated at some 20,000 people, and at the gates of the cemetery a moving oration by Franz Grillparzer was read out. It was a fitting tribute to a man who had achieved so much through his music. He had excelled in all the main genres of the time. His music expressed the complete range of human emotions, and at exceptional depth. His compositional methods, in which a single passage might be drafted over thirty times, exhibit incredible intensity of thought combined with ingenuity of technique. The complexity of his ideas has provided an inexhaustible fascination for modern commentators. And his originality extended the bounds of his art in numerous different directions.

Life after death

Since Beethoven's death his music has lived on in innumerable performances throughout the world, and his name has become a byword for the archetypal great composer and artistic genius. His impact on his successors for the whole of the nineteenth century and well into the twentieth has been immense. Many composers have paid direct homage to his ideas in their own works, whether in programmatic symphonies that took Beethoven's *Pastoral* as their initial inspiration, in pure symphonies such as those of Brahms and Bruckner, in song cycles that look back to *An die ferne Geliebte*, or in many other genres. His Ninth Symphony, meanwhile, has been used or misused for numerous political ends, whether by the Nazis, the Japanese, or the European Union, the last of which has adopted the main theme of the symphony's finale as its official anthem (but without Schiller's words, since this would prioritize one language over the others in the Union). A statue was erected in his honour in his native city of Bonn in 1845, and the city still hails him today

---

[23] See Christian Reiter, 'The Causes of Beethoven's Death and his Locks of Hair: A Forensic-Toxicological Investigation', trans. Michael Lorenz, *The Beethoven Journal*, 22 (2007), pp. 2–5; 'Letters to the Editor', *The Beethoven Journal*, 22 (2007), pp. 124–5; Josef Eisinger, 'Was Beethoven Lead-Poisoned?', *The Beethoven Journal*, 23 (2008), pp. 15–17.

23. *Beethoven's funeral procession of 29 March 1827, in a painting by Franz Stöber. In the background can be seen the Schwarzspanierhaus, where rooms on the top floor formed Beethoven's main residence from October 1825 until his death.*

as its most famous son. Romanticized pictures of him were being painted for many years after his death, and his image can also be found in recent times on objects as diverse as postage stamps and (more appropriately) the labels of alcoholic drinks. Several films have been made about his life, though with greatly varying degrees of accuracy, while literature on his music is enormous and rapidly expanding, as scholars find a seemingly inexhaustible supply of interesting ideas hidden beneath the surface of the notes. It is the enduring power and forcefulness of his music, however, that is perhaps his most remarkable legacy. Its intellectual courage and emotional depth have been strong enough to save several people from attempted suicide in well-attested cases, just as Beethoven himself had been saved from suicide by his art, according to his own statement in his Heiligenstadt Testament. Many people are aware that he composed great music, but few realize just how great it is, intellectually and emotionally.

Beethoven's legacy is all the more remarkable when it is remembered that he was operating against a background of profound deafness and frequent bouts of ill health, as well as frequent incomprehension of, and hostility to, some of his most original creations. His 'life' since his death in 1827 has been in some ways even more extraordinary than his everyday life in Vienna was, and his aim of achieving immortality, in the Greek sense of lasting fame, has been well and truly realized. His integrity, generosity, and nobility of spirit were much admired by those who knew him best, and he was surely confident of achieving immortality in the Christian sense as well as the Greek sense, as is evident in the *Missa solemnis* at his awe-inspiring setting of the words 'and the life of the world to come'.

Beethoven and his nephew:
the appeal memorandum

One of Beethoven's most extraordinary creations was his appeal memorandum of February 1820. It was the last and much the longest document he produced in connection with the protracted dispute (outlined above in Chapters Four and Five) concerning the guardianship of his nephew Karl, and it was written with great passion, since it concerned something even more important to him than his music: Karl's welfare. It is dated 18 February 1820 at the end, but it is so long (forty-eight pages in his handwriting – the longest prose document he ever wrote) that it must have been begun some days before then, and its five main subheadings were mentioned in a letter to his lawyer Johann Baptist Bach about a week earlier. It was intended as the basis of his appeal to have his sister-in-law Johanna (whom he refers to as 'Fr. B.' – Frau Beethoven) excluded from the guardianship on the grounds that she was wholly unsuitable. The document itself was not submitted but was instead sent to Johann Baptist Bach. Beethoven then asked his friend Carl Joseph Bernard to reword it thoroughly and more concisely, so as to make a more forceful impression on the judges,[1] and the case was considered some weeks later, on 29 March.

The memorandum is very roughly written and not nearly as neat as the Heiligenstadt Testament. There are numerous deletions, as well as several insertions either between lines or at the foot of a page, and one leaf (pp. 7–8) is missing. The memorandum is divided into six sections, but each section consists of more or less uninterrupted prose; sentences are concluded by a comma, a semicolon, a dash, or occasionally a series of exclamation marks, but hardly ever a full stop, and there is no division into separate paragraphs. Beethoven frequently underlines a word or phrase, but these underlinings have little significance beyond indicating something of the energy and vehemence with which he wrote.

The original document can currently be viewed in the digital archives of the Beethoven-Haus website, and a complete translation appears in Emily Anderson's edition of Beethoven's

---

[1] A-1006, 1007; BB-1366, 1367.

letters.[2] A selection of the main passages is given below (in a translation that differs slightly from Anderson's), with some brief commentary. Modern punctuation and paragraph layout have been used, and the rather irregular underlinings have been omitted, partly because the sentence structure in English often differs from the German, so that no exact underlining is possible. The memorandum begins with a list of the six sections before proceeding under each heading in turn, as follows.

[1.] Information about Fr. B.
[2.]   "   the guardianship panel of the *Magistrat* about my nephew
[3.]   "   my nephew and his school reports
[4.]   "   what I have done for my nephew
[5.]   "   his property
[6.] Addendum

It is painful for someone like me to have to sully himself in the least with a person like Fr. B. But since this is my last attempt to save my nephew, for his sake I am allowing this humiliation. – *lite abstine, nam vincens, multum amiseris* [refrain from litigation, for even if you win you will have lost much]. I should much rather follow this precept, but the welfare of a third person prevents me from doing so.

Fr. B. had no education whatsoever; her parents, upholsterers by profession, left her mostly to herself. Thus corruptible tendencies already developed in her early years; when still living in her parents' house she had to appear before the police court, because she accused her maid of an offence of which she was the culprit, and the maid was found completely blameless. But the police acquitted her out of consideration when she promised to improve. In 1811, when she was already a wife and mother, though indeed highly frivolous, of easy virtue, stubborn and malicious, and had already partly lost her good reputation, she committed a new and more dreadful atrocity, which even brought her before the criminal court. Here too she watched calmly when wholly blameless people were being associated with her atrocity. Finally she had to agree that she was the sole offender; only through the greatest efforts of her

---

[2] www.beethoven-haus-bonn.de; Emily Anderson (trans. and ed.), *The Letters of Beethoven*, 3 vols (London: Macmillan, 1961), pp. 1388–1408.

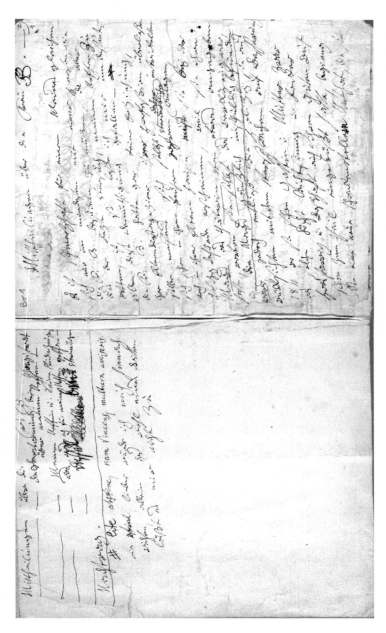

24. *The first two sides of Beethoven's appeal memorandum. The first page lists the contents, and also includes a passage to be inserted on the right-hand page at the # sign on line 7. For translation see p. 138.*

husband and my friends was she, though not unpunished, yet exempted from the severest punishment and again released.

This dreadful event brought to my late brother a serious illness, from which he had to lead the life of an invalid; only through my charitable support was his life still spared for a while. Even some time before his death she withdrew a considerable sum of money, unknown to him; this made him want to separate from her, but the Reaper came, and separated him from – life on 15 November 1815. The day before his death, while thanking me in his will as his benefactor, he nominated me sole guardian of his son. On the same day I had scarcely left him for a few hours when on my return my brother told me that during my absence something had been added, which he had been misled into signing. (It was the codicil in which she had herself nominated as guardian on the same level as myself.) He bade me recover this at once from the lawyer, but the latter could not be found that day, even though at my brother's bidding I went several times to his house. The next day at 5 o'clock in the morning my brother died. Despite this, only one witness was lacking to prove that my brother wished to have this codicil destroyed, even though through Paragraph 191 of the Civil Code it already held no force, and the Worshipful *Landrecht* also ascribed to it no legal validity, in that they have confirmed my appointment as sole guardian. It is clear that in 1815 she had still not taken any steps towards her moral improvement. For after what I have said, her dishonesty towards her son was revealed concerning the inventory. I said nothing, for I wanted only to save the soul of my nephew.

The allegation that Johanna's crime of 1811 caused her husband Carl to become ill is clearly without foundation, except inasmuch as the stress of the police investigation and subsequent court case could have lowered his resistance to infection. There is no reason to doubt the substance of any of Beethoven's other claims, however. The confusion over the codicil, discussed earlier (see p. 104), inevitably caused dispute, and Carl's true wishes when he was at death's door cannot be ascertained. Nevertheless, Paragraph 191 of the Civil Code stipulated that anyone convicted of a crime, as Johanna had been, was deemed unsuitable for guardianship, and this law was one of the main planks of Beethoven's attempts to debar her. Her lifestyle as described by him, had his description been proved correct, would also have debarred her, and it showed no sign of improvement after Carl's death, as Beethoven then proceeds to indicate.

Immediately after the death of my brother she had intimate relations with a lover, which shocked even the modesty of her innocent son. She was to be found in all the dance halls and at festivities, while her son was not even given basic necessities, and was abandoned to some wretched maid of hers. What would have become of him if I had not taken interest in him?! That she still from 1815 to 1820 showed herself to be just as much a rotten, highly deceitful person, duplicitous in the highest degree, is proved by the following: whenever she could, wherever my nephew happened to be, either at my home or at his boarding school, she sought to bring forward wrong ideas, and always through secret engagements to induce him to appalling dissimulation himself. She sought to corrupt him even with money, and gave him further money to misuse other people for her evil ends. A few times when he had behaved very badly, she contrived to invite him to her home, where it was then made out that such behaviour did not matter at all. She sought through the most appalling intrigues, plots, and defamations to disparage me, his benefactor, nourisher, and support, in short his father in the true sense of the word, and to infect everyone, even the most innocent, with her moral poison.

Finally her hellish and yet stupid activities reached a new highpoint under the worthy guardianship panel [Obervormundschaft] of the Magistrat, in that at the approaching Easter examinations in 1819 she urged my nephew to arrange that he come in the second or third class, so that he could not be sent away from here. Yet with me she had always found a barrier, which she tried in vain to demolish. But as a guardian Herr von Tuscher was rarely listened to or given attention by the guardianship panel of the Magistrat. They took particular delight in enjoying a few hellish meals with that charming woman, and therefore my nephew has her to thank forever that he has wasted a whole year of his educational life because of the attachment which this worthy guardianship panel had formed for his most loving mother. As one can imagine, this guardianship panel supported their favourites as they deserved; thus we see her as guardian of her son from October 1819 till now in February 1820, humiliating the true and sole guardian, benefactor, provider, and support of his late brother and father of my nephew, as of my nephew himself, in the lowest and most vulgar way.

The suggestion that the guardianship panel fraternized with Johanna over shared meals seems particularly alarming, and perhaps helps to explain why they had ruled in her favour.

The next section of the memorandum provides information about the guardianship panel and their partiality, and how they believed Johanna's false accusation that Beethoven had advised his nephew against going to confession with a priest, whereas in fact he had done the opposite and later took Karl to confession himself. Because of his hearing difficulty Beethoven then had to nominate a co-guardian. He continues:

I chose Herr von Tuscher as guardian of my nephew, and both in this situation and in general I did not want to keep him at home; for in these circumstances my cares were too great. Thus in March 1819 he went to Herr Kudlich's institute; but I was not very keen on this and would rather have had him at Giannatasio's. But it was known that the views of the latter were against the mother, in that he considered the removal of her from her son to be the uppermost factor in the education of my nephew; and it was preferred that he should be placed where the mother should perhaps receive a more favourable treatment. Although I was bearing the costs as before, I had to let this happen, for I was no longer the guardian. Meanwhile I had received an offer from the renowned, worthy scholar and priest J. M. Sailer to take my nephew into his home at Landshut, and to lead the supervision of his education. The worthy Abbot of St Michael described this as the greatest piece of luck that could befall my nephew; and other enlightened men said the same. Even His Imperial Highness the present Archbishop of Olmütz concurred and gave his support. Herr von Tuscher agreed with this plan and thought it the best, since my nephew would through his removal from here be wholly prevented from breaking any more the commandment 'Honour thy father and mother' (to which he was always being directed), which in her presence was impossible to observe. Although the boy knew his mother perfectly well from childhood, yet the avoidance of everything offensive would certainly be more desirable; moreover, he would thereby be completely removed from the disturbances of his mother. However, this could not be done without the consent of the guardianship panel. Hence they were approached; and imagine, what logic, what principles, what philosophy!! The mother was now invited to protest against it!!! In short, the whole plan fell through. Herr von Tuscher was now considered prejudiced. To the Referent who had finally got to know Fr. B. perfectly well and also regarded the removal of her son as for the best, another Referent was attached. But he too was accused of prejudice and therefore he himself resigned the position. During this period my nephew could leave the institute whenever he liked; the mother had free access, and my nephew became outwardly and inwardly so changed that he was no longer recognizable. And now it happened that the mother gave advice to arrange that he come in the second or third class, whereby he could not be sent away from here. This he did, and must now stay put in the same class for another whole year.

Here one can sense the desperate nature of a struggle, so common even today, between an individual and mindless, stupid bureaucracy that is incapable of perceiving the whole picture. The plan mentioned here was for Karl to be sent to a school at Landshut in Bavaria, overseen by the eminent theologian and future bishop Johann Michael Sailer. Sailer was a friend of Antonie Brentano, and when Beethoven discovered this he wrote to her asking her to contact Sailer to see if he would agree to Karl being sent there. Sailer approved and replied to Beethoven direct. The plan received widespread support, particularly from the 'worthy Abbot of St Michael', Father Ignatius Thomas, who said, as reported in Beethoven's conversation book: 'If I thought for 100 years, I could not imagine anything better than to send the boy to Prof. Sailer's.'[3] Support also came from Beethoven's friend Archduke Rudolph, here referred to by his new title as Archbishop of Olmütz. But the plan was resisted by Johanna and therefore rejected.

---

[3] BKh, vol. 1, p. 72.

Both sides of the dispute regarded the fourth commandment from Scripture, 'Honour thy father and mother', as important, and one of Johanna's main claims was that Beethoven had encouraged Karl to break it by speaking ill of her. Beethoven's view, as can be seen, was that he believed the commandment should be observed in principle, but that it was 'impossible to observe' when what Karl said dishonoured her but was nevertheless perfectly true. Whether she urged Karl to fail his examinations is less certain, but this may have heightened his later apprehension about examinations, which was one factor that led to his suicide attempt in August 1826.

In the next passage Beethoven outlines events since Easter 1819, recording how Karl fell ill through overeating and drinking during a visit to Johanna's and was afterwards placed at Joseph Blöchlinger's boarding school. Tuscher resigned the guardianship, and it was allocated to Johanna and one Leopold Nussböck, though Beethoven continued to pay all the expenses of the boarding school.

In the third section of the memorandum Beethoven summarizes Karl's progress at school, and then proceeds to the fourth section, 'what I have done for my nephew'.

> For five years I have largely at my own expense paid for his education and provided for him as few fathers would. In all situations I have never abandoned the true aim: to train my nephew to be a capable, skilled, and civilized citizen. When I was guardian and equally when I was not, and even now when I am fighting about this, I carry on and ensure my nephew's wellbeing. For two years, from 1816 to 1818, he was at Giannatasio's institute entirely at my expense, where he had his own piano teacher as extra, had a hernia operation, and a special legal trustee was engaged for him here and in Prague. Also I travelled to Retz concerning his property etc. etc. These two years can probably be reckoned as 4000 florins WW; the accounts could easily be produced if necessary. Only then did the first contribution come, as can be seen in more detail in the information about his property. During the time he was with me, and then in Kudlich's institute from March 1819 until his departure from the institute, it cost at least 2000 florins WW. On 22 June 1819 he entered Herr Blöchlinger's institute. Since these are actually the shortest accounts, I attach these as Supplement C. Additionally many other necessities such

as clothes, illnesses etc. are not accounted for at all. There will be few uncles and guardians in the kingdom who provide so generously for their dependants, and so completely unselfishly. At least I have no other intention than to regard myself as the originator of something good and to shape a better human nature.

The currency referred to here is *Wiener Währung* (Viennese currency), paper money in which a florin was worth 40 per cent of a silver florin (silver florins had been withdrawn from circulation in 1809 in the midst of rampant inflation, but were reintroduced gradually in 1818 and had not greatly changed in value). Beethoven's annuity was 3,400 florins WW, or 1,360 silver florins per annum, which was more or less sufficient to pay for his own expenses but could not cover Karl's. Thus Beethoven had had to pay for these out of earnings from publications, and he was justified in pointing out that he had been extremely generous over this. Not until 1818 was any contribution to Karl's upkeep made either by Johanna or from funds from Karl's own inheritance.

The fifth section of the document provides details about how much money was being provided for Karl and from what sources, and it is followed by an auxiliary 'conclusion' which acts rather like a coda to one of Beethoven's compositions, bringing together the implications and consequences of what has previously been said, so as to make a fitting culmination and sense of closure.

I must admit I am tired out, and if one must suffer out of goodwill, I believe I have certainly done so here. It is high time that Fr. B. be put back in her place through the High Court of Appeal, and know that no intrigues can overthrow any more what has been ruled and established by the Worshipful *Landrecht*. For she has already pursued for at least four years this plan to have her son with her and have guardianship over him. She must therefore be placed quite out of reach of harming him. Only then can humanity and consideration of her rights be brought to bear – although this was always the case for me in respect of her, except where the welfare of my nephew demanded that her obstinacy should be overcome through the law. Yet she has never been willing to accept either consideration or magnanimity or true kindness.

Nobody should believe her claim that I am secretly led by hatred or revenge against her. It is painful for me to have to speak of her, and were it not for my nephew I would never think of her, nor speak of her, nor operate against her. May the High Court of Appeal now grant my plea, and decide whether Fr. B. and the municipal sequestrator Nussböck should receive the guardianship of my nephew, or I, the guardian appointed in the will (with a co-guardian, Herr von Peters, chosen by me and very agreeable to me and useful to my nephew), who have been the benefactor, support, and provider for my nephew for five years. The decision will bring my nephew wellbeing or, if it goes against me, absolutely certain disaster. For my nephew needs me, not I him ...

Should I also as a human being have failed at times, or indeed should my hearing come into question, yet a child is not taken away from his father for these two reasons. And I have throughout been a father to my nephew, just as I was a benefactor to his father. God bless my work; I lay the wellbeing and prospects of an orphan at the heart and wisdom of the High Court of Appeal.

Beethoven closed this section with a Latin quotation, but later he added a supplement on some extra pages. This addendum (with the date at the end) repeats some of the points already made, and provides a few additional details about certain episodes in the dispute.

It is easy today to criticize Beethoven and the Appeal Court for removing Karl from his mother, but even today children can be and occasionally are removed from parents deemed unsuitable. Some observers have also challenged Beethoven's claim 'my nephew needs me, not I him', and suggested that Beethoven's need for someone to love him was actually greater than Karl's need for protection; but this seems a strained reading of the evidence. What emerges from the memorandum is Beethoven's fundamental belief that he must do his very best to make Karl an excellent and well-educated citizen, and that this was a higher calling even than composing great music, for he knew he was the only person who could protect Karl from whatever bad influence his mother may have had. Karl's personal happiness seems to have been of little concern by comparison; so too was Beethoven's own personal comfort, as he tired himself out and expended large sums of money to further his cause. Johanna's happiness also was a minor consideration at best. Beethoven repeatedly indicated that he had nothing against her and had tried to treat her gently, but she had not responded appropriately nor reformed her ways at all, and continued to pose a danger to Karl's development. What is most significant is that even her supporters did not try to dispute this or defend her character, but merely attacked Beethoven for his deafness and such matters as his willingness to let Karl say bad things about Johanna. Beethoven, meanwhile, displayed unbounded generosity towards Karl, a strong sense of morality based on his religious beliefs, and extraordinary determination to accomplish something worthwhile. In this respect, the appeal memorandum and Beethoven's compositions are founded on the same underlying principles and attitudes, and show something of the same energy in their creation.

SIX

MYTHS ABOUT BEETHOVEN

Early myths

Beethoven's extraordinary life – that of a deaf musician who defied the odds to become the most celebrated composer of his day, combining highly idiosyncratic composing methods with an inexhaustible fund of ideas, and possessing lofty moral ideals and ambitions alongside a disordered everyday existence – well illustrates the old adage that truth is stranger than fiction. Nevertheless, many accounts of his life have been written that are coloured by fiction and inaccuracy, whether through error, wild speculation, or deliberate deception, or through attempts to write biography only loosely based on his actual life and containing much acknowledged invention.[1] Thus numerous myths have grown up in and around Beethoven biography. Some have long been dispelled, but others have an attractiveness so persistent that they still remain in circulation.

These myths began at an early date. Beethoven was for many years unsure of the year of his birth (1770), and his confusion was increased by the fact that his older brother, also called Ludwig (Ludwig Maria), had died on 8 April 1769 only six days after his birth. Thus Beethoven tended to assume that the baby born in 1770 was Ludwig Maria, while he himself was born one or two years later. When he was sent a copy of his baptismal certificate in June 1810 it correctly showed the date 17 December 1770, but Beethoven wrote on the back: '1772: The baptismal certificate seems to be incorrect, since there was a Ludwig born before me ...'[2] The date of

---

[1] Recent fictional biographies include John Suchet, *The Last Master ... A Fictional Biography of Ludwig van Beethoven*, 3 vols (London: Little, Brown, 1996–8); and Susan Lund, *Raptus: A Novel about Beethoven* (Melbourn, Herts.: Melstamps, 1995). There are also films about Beethoven's life that include varying and often large amounts of fiction, such as Bernard Rose's *Immortal Beloved* (1994). For an indication of its unreliability, see Donald F. Sloane, 'A Multiple-Choice Quiz on the Historical Accuracy of Bernard Rose's *Immortal Beloved*', *The Beethoven Journal*, 10 (1995), pp. 30–1 (followed by further comments from various contributors on pp. 32–9).

[2] TF, pp. 52–4.

1772 was widely circulated, for it appeared in Ernst Ludwig Gerber's *Historisch-biographisches Lexicon der Tonkünstler* (1790–92), the standard reference work of the day concerning musicians.[3] It then reappeared in the first published book about Beethoven, a biography by Johann Aloys Schlosser based partly on Gerber and published only a few months after the composer's death.[4] Only fresh examination of the baptismal registers in Bonn, which showed the two Ludwigs born in 1769 and 1770, was able to dispel the myth.

Schlosser's account includes a few other errors, but it is not nearly as inaccurate as has generally been assumed (its alleged worthlessness is another myth hard to dispel), and it does correct some myths about Beethoven. The most notable one concerns a spider: Beethoven supposedly befriended one as a child, and fell unconscious with shock when one day his aunt killed the spider, remaining on the brink of death for three months afterwards. This anecdote was printed in the widely respected journal *Allgemeine musikalische Zeitung*, but Schlosser was able to confirm that the child in question was not Beethoven but the violinist and composer (Isidore) Berthaume (*c.*1752–1802), with the similarity of name having caused the confusion.[5]

More recent myths

One of the most frequent sources for myths about Beethoven is his deafness. For a start, the extent of his deafness has often been exaggerated. He was still able to hear tolerably well until he was over 40, and was using ear-trumpets to assist him after 1813. Even at the very end of his life he was never totally deaf. Although the fact that he became increasingly hard of hearing over a long period is not in doubt, the cause of the deafness has given rise to much ill-informed speculation. Schlosser asserts that the probable cause was 'the unusual sensitivity of the various parts of his hearing mechanism',[6] which modern science has shown to be completely implausible. Beethoven's own explanations are equally unconvincing: in his first mention he notes that his deafness is said to be due to his abdomen, which had always been in a poor state.[7] On another occasion he relates that he became so angry on one occasion that he jumped up and threw himself on the floor; 'When I arose again I found myself deaf and have

---

[3] Ernst Ludwig Gerber, *Historisch-biographisches Lexicon der Tonkünstler (1790–1792)*, ed. Othmar Wessely (Graz: Akademische Druck- und Verlagsanstalt, 1977), col. 156.

[4] Johann Aloys Schlosser, *Ludwig van Beethoven: Eine Biographie desselben, verbunden mit Urtheilen über seine Werke* (Prague: Buchler, Stephani and Schlosser, 1828 [Sept. 1827]). English version in *Beethoven: The First Biography [1827]*, trans. Reinhard G. Pauly, ed. Barry Cooper (Portland, OR: Amadeus, 1996).

[5] Ibid., pp. 42–6.

[6] Ibid., p. 85.

[7] A-51; BB-65 (29 June 1801).

remained so ever since.'[8] Another fanciful explanation was that his deafness became much worse from around 1812 as a result of Antonie Brentano's daughter playfully pouring a bottle of ice-cold water on his head.[9] Several other possible causes of deafness, suggested by various writers, have since been shown to be implausible in Beethoven's case, such as Whipple's Disease, Paget's Disease, lead poisoning, and otitis media. Otosclerosis has been widely suggested, but there are difficulties with this hypothesis too, since the autopsy apparently indicated nerve deafness rather than disease of the bone. The theory that the deafness was an after-effect of typhus fever seems to hold most credence.[10] What is most extraordinary about the myths concerning Beethoven's deafness is that, despite a detailed autopsy performed at his death, and despite nearly 200 years of further medical advances, the precise cause has stubbornly resisted firm identification.

The effects of Beethoven's deafness also gave rise to myths, at least in his later years and shortly thereafter. Many people attributed the supposed harshness of his late style to his inability to hear music properly any more. Most prominent among these critics was his former pupil Carl Czerny, who asserted that during Beethoven's third period he 'became completely deaf', and that this was 'the cause of the uncomfortable keyboard writing in his last piano pieces', as well as 'the reason for many harsh harmonies'.[11] Although the deafness probably had some effect on certain details in Beethoven's style (his music may have become more cerebral and less improvisatory as a result of his declining tendency to try things out at the piano as his deafness increased), it seems improbable that he could not judge accurately the effect of his harmony, or the awkwardness of his keyboard writing. Czerny is even further off the mark in his claim that the first movements of Beethoven's last two piano sonatas, Opp. 110 and 111, were composed much earlier than the following movements. Beethoven's sketchbooks, which have been examined in detail since Czerny's day, show unequivocally that none of the movements of these sonatas was begun until 1821, long after some of the works that Czerny correctly identified as third-period. He was equally wrong in claiming that Beethoven 'could still hear' when composing the first three movements of the Ninth Symphony (which date mainly from 1823) but 'was deaf' when he wrote the choral finale.[12]

---

[8] TDR, vol. 2, p. 168.
[9] Carl Czerny, *On the Proper Performance of All Beethoven's Works for the Piano*, ed. Paul Badura-Skoda (Vienna: Universal Edition, 1970), p. 11.
[10] This suggestion comes originally from Beethoven's friend Aloys Weissenbach, a surgeon, and has been frequently repeated; see TF, pp. 252–3. See also Davies, *Beethoven in Person*, pp. 135–63, for a comprehensive overview of the various theories and their difficulties.
[11] Czerny, ed. Badura-Skoda, *On the Proper Performance*, p. 9.
[12] Ibid., pp. 9–12.

Beethoven's deafness is also partly to blame for the popular misconception of him as an isolated and aloof figure, since his detachment from society was initially caused by his attempts around 1800 to conceal his deafness. He quickly became aware of this misunderstanding, as he indicated at the beginning of his Heiligenstadt Testament of October 1802 (see p. 57). Since this document was not published until after his death, the misapprehension that he was 'hostile, stubborn, or misanthropic' towards the world at large had plenty of opportunity to gain currency, and little chance of correction. Hence it has never been completely dispelled from popular consciousness.

Beethoven's attitude to Haydn has given rise to further myths. On the basis of a few shreds of somewhat ambivalent evidence, various writers have constructed scenarios in which it has been assumed that the two composers were temperamentally unsuited to each other and had frequent disagreements. Examination of the sources, however, indicates that any animosity went no further than 'mutual distrust and feelings of ambivalence', which were confined mainly to the period 1800–4.[13] In other respects Beethoven found Haydn a helpful teacher (he remained with him for over a year, until Haydn left Vienna for London) and a kind companion (Haydn lent him money when needed, and they drank coffee and chocolate together in 1793), and he gladly dedicated his first Viennese piano sonatas to him.

Beethoven's relationships with women have inevitably come in for much myth-making. It has been alleged that he had syphilis or some other venereal disease, and that he made use of prostitutes at times. These claims cannot be disproved – it is virtually impossible to prove a negative of this type – but there is absolutely no real evidence to support either claim; all the evidence is flimsy and circumstantial, and one must conclude that in all probability they are myths. For example, Beethoven referred mysteriously to 'fortresses' in a series of letters to Nikolaus Zmeskall, but the suggestion that this is a code word for 'prostitutes' is wildly speculative and improbable, although it has been transmitted as fact by several writers. Beethoven was not in the habit of using such code words in his letters; and even if the suggestion were correct it is clear from the letters that he intended to keep clear of the 'fortresses'. On another occasion he was asked: 'Where did you go today around 7 o'clock by the Haarmarkt hunting for girls?' This too has been used as evidence that he was looking for prostitutes, but the implication came from the questioner, not from Beethoven, and in fact he was almost certainly hunting not for girls but

---

[13] See James Webster, 'The Falling-Out between Haydn and Beethoven: The Evidence of the Sources', in Lewis Lockwood and Phyllis Benjamin (eds.), *Beethoven Essays: Studies in Honor of Elliot Forbes* (Cambridge, MA: Harvard University Press, 1984), pp. 3–45.

for Matthias Tuscher, whose address (682 Haarmarkt) he had noted down only about a day earlier.[14]

Another myth about Beethoven's relationship with women is that he hated his sister-in-law Johanna. His writings, both private and to other people, make it perfectly plain that he held no such feelings.[15] The woman who has generated most fictional writing about Beethoven, however, is undoubtedly the one he addressed in a letter of July 1812 as his 'Immortal Beloved'. Early suggestions as to her identity included Giulietta (Julie) Guicciardi and Amalie Sebald, which have been shown to be impossible. But even since 1972, when Maynard Solomon appeared to have demonstrated that she was Antonie Brentano, there have been elaborate attempts to prove that the Immortal Beloved was some other woman: Josephine Deym (advocated by Tellenbach and others), Marie Erdödy (Altman), Almerie Esterházy (Celeda), or Bettina Brentano (Walden).[16] At least three of these suggestions must be incorrect, and there are strong counter-arguments against all four; most scholars still support the Antonie Brentano hypothesis. As with Beethoven's deafness, however, it is remarkable that there has been such an array of alternative hypotheses, with evidence sufficient to engender much reasoned argument but insufficient for definite proof.

Schindler as creator of myths

Although the myth-makers are therefore still hard at work, the biggest myth-maker of all is undoubtedly Anton Schindler. He was in contact with Beethoven from 1822 and possibly a little earlier, but he made out in a biography published in 1840 and largely rewritten for a new edition in 1860 that he had known Beethoven since 1814,[17] and that he had spent much time in private with him, discussing aspects of many of his major works. To bolster his claim to intimate acquaintance with Beethoven, Schindler began after Beethoven's death to insert wholly fictitious conversations into the conversation books that Beethoven had been using. Many of these books still had small blank spaces or even completely blank pages, and so it was not hard for Schindler to insert additional material to suit his purposes. For many years these forgeries remained undetected, and they were brought to light only in the 1970s. Altogether there are over 250 fake conversations, containing nearly 700 separate 'speeches'

---

[14] BKh, vol. 1, pp. 254 and 253.

[15] Cooper, *Beethoven*, p. 255 (2nd edn, p. 275).

[16] Marie-Elisabeth Tellenbach, *Beethoven und seine 'unsterbliche Geliebte' Josephine Brunswick* (Zurich: Atlantis, 1983); Gail Altman, *Beethoven: A Man of his Word* (Tallahassee, FL: Anubian Press, 1996); Jaroslav Celeda, 'Beethoven's "Immortal Beloved"', ed. Oldrich Pulkert, rev. Hans-Werner Küthen, trans. William Meredith, *The Beethoven Journal*, 15 (2000), pp. 2–18; Edward Walden, *Beethoven's Immortal Beloved: Solving the Mystery* (Lanham, MD: Scarecrow Press, 2011).

[17] The 1860 edition has appeared in English as Anton Schindler, *Beethoven as I Knew Him*, trans. Constance Jolly, ed. Donald MacArdle (London: Faber & Faber, 1966).

by Schindler. Many are interspersed with genuine conversations that Schindler had with Beethoven, though the genuine ones date only from November 1822 onwards, thus indicating that the two men were not properly acquainted before then. (Schindler is not to blame, however, for the myth that around 400 conversation books originally survived, and that he destroyed more than half of them, although he did claim to have destroyed a few pages – which may or may not be true.)

The forged conversations often contain discussion about Beethoven's music. In one of the latest, for example, Schindler comments, 'You are very well today, so we can poetize something e.g. about the B flat major Trio [Op. 97], where we were recently interrupted.' After a more general discussion that includes references to Aristotle, Euripides, Faust, and Shakespeare, Schindler comes round to the said trio: 'The first movement dreams of open happiness and contentment. Also mischievousness, cheerful playfulness and obstinacy (Beethovenian) are there.' He then continues with similar comments about the next two movements.[18] These and similar insertions were written to convince the world that he was on very close terms with Beethoven and had been given detailed and special insights into the music, and in this he succeeded until many years after his death. It is now clear, however, that every single one of Schindler's many discussions of the content of the music that appear in the conversation books is fictitious. All his genuine conversations, by contrast, are of practical, everyday matters such as copying of parts or looking for lodgings. The above 'conversation', for example, which was inserted into a book dating from February 1827 when Beethoven was extremely ill, immediately follows a typical genuine comment: 'He showed me the register, where I saw all your instructions for receipts together.'

Having apparently proved his specialized insights into Beethoven's compositions and his long and close association with the composer, Schindler felt confident about inventing anecdotes that amplify the background of several of Beethoven's major works. These anecdotes are still widely circulated as if they were fact, but it is almost certain that all are pure invention. It was Schindler who claimed that the idea for a symphony dedicated to Napoleon (what became the *Eroica*) was suggested by General Bernadotte; he bolstered his claim by referring to a letter that Beethoven wrote in 1823, but the letter in question makes no reference to the symphony. Regarding the Triple Concerto, Schindler claimed it was written for Archduke Rudolph, but this seems highly unlikely since the archduke would have been only 16 at the time (1804) and did not have any documented contact with Beethoven until over three years later. The famous description of the opening of the Fifth Symphony, 'Thus Fate knocks at the door' (or more accurately, '... pounds at the portal'), is

---

[18] BKh, vol. 11, pp. 203–5.

another apparent invention of Schindler, who claimed that Beethoven had said these words in his presence. For the *Pastoral* Symphony, Schindler related a long anecdote about how the two of them visited Heiligenstadt in April 1823, with Beethoven telling him that the slow movement quotes the calls of not three birds but four, the fourth being a 'Goldammer' (usually understood to mean a yellowhammer).[19] Schindler provided quite a lot of circumstantial detail, but every detail that can be checked proves to be incorrect.[20] For example, the conversation books show that the two men visited Hetzendorf, not Heiligenstadt, in April 1823. Thus the entire anecdote appears to be a complete fabrication.

For the Eighth Symphony, Schindler constructed an even more elaborate hoax. He claimed that the ticking figure that accompanies much of the second movement related to Maelzel's newly invented metronome, and that the movement was based on a canon that Beethoven had composed in Maelzel's honour: 'Ta ta ta ta … lieber, lieber Maelzel' (WoO 162). To corroborate his claim he inserted fictitious entries in two separate conversation books, and even composed the canon on which the movement was supposedly based.[21] His account contains all sorts of chronological difficulties, not least the fact that the word 'Metronom', which appears in the canon, had not been coined when the Eighth Symphony was composed.

When someone goes to such lengths to fabricate evidence, it becomes difficult to accept anything they say unless there is independent confirmation. Hence Schindler's other statements about underlying ideas for Beethoven's compositions must surely be untrue. A particularly noted case concerns two piano sonatas, Op. 31 No. 2 in D minor and Op. 57 in F minor. Schindler claims he asked Beethoven for the meaning of these and was told: 'Just read Shakespeare's *Tempest*.'[22] Plausible though this is, like most of Schindler's anecdotes, it is surely another invention, and has unfortunately led to the D minor sonata becoming nicknamed the 'Tempest' Sonata. Similarly Schindler's claim about a different sonata, Op. 90, dedicated to Count Moritz Lichnowsky, can be summarily dismissed. Here Schindler claims that Beethoven said its two movements depicted the count's love for his second wife Josepha; but Schindler rather undermines his credibility with some inaccurate details, stating that the count fell in love with her 'after the death of his first wife' and married her in 1816. In actual fact the first wife did not die until 1817, the second marriage took place in 1820, and the second wife had given birth to the

---

[19] Schindler, ed. MacArdle, *Beethoven*, pp. 112 (*Eroica*), 140 (Triple Concerto), 146 (Fifth Symphony), 144–5 (*Pastoral*).
[20] See Barry Cooper, 'Schindler and the *Pastoral* Symphony', *The Beethoven Newsletter*, 8 (1993), pp. 2–6.
[21] See Standley Howell, 'Beethoven's Maelzel Canon: Another Schindler Forgery?', *The Musical Times*, 120 (1979), pp. 987–90.
[22] Schindler, ed. MacArdle, *Beethoven*, p. 406.

count's illegitimate child in 1814, the year the sonata was composed.[23] It seems completely implausible to suggest that Beethoven would want to portray an embarrassing extramarital affair in a piano sonata.

Schindler's 'explanations' of Beethoven's works are actually not the most extreme example of this approach. For this we must turn to Arnold Schering, who in the 1930s published several books and articles in which he claimed that Beethoven based his instrumental works on various plays, poems, and legends.[24] Schering claimed that the *Eroica* was based on scenes from Homer's *Iliad*, while the 'Waldstein' Sonata described scenes from the *Odyssey*. For other compositions, works by such writers as Goethe, Schiller, Cervantes, and Shakespeare were invoked. Schering produced no evidence to support his wild speculations, however, apart from references to his own thought processes, which had allegedly unlocked these secrets, and thankfully few later writers have accepted his claims or followed this approach.

Another oft-cited story by Schindler relates how he visited Beethoven in August 1819 to find him 'singing, yelling, stamping his feet' as he composed the fugue in the Credo of the *Missa solemnis*, and with 'his features distorted to the point of inspiring terror. He looked as though he had just engaged in a life and death struggle with the whole army of contrapuntists, his everlasting enemies.'[25] This vivid and appealing but fanciful description comes from a period when Schindler had no known connection with Beethoven; moreover Beethoven's sketchbooks and conversation books show that as late as March 1820 he had reached only the middle of the Credo, and that he did not begin wrestling with the contrapuntal intricacies of its final fugue until some time later, thus long after August 1819. Schindler is not to blame, however, for the widely circulated myth that Schiller's *An die Freude* (To Joy) in the Ninth Symphony was covertly intended as an ode to freedom.

Misrepresentations of Beethoven's output

Besides offering background 'explanations' of some works, Schindler also claimed that Beethoven wrote a set of dances for a band near Mödling in summer 1819.[26] A set of dances (WoO 17) was discovered in Leipzig in 1905 that vaguely matches Schindler's description, and so it has sometimes been assumed that these are the said dances. But the Leipzig dances show no clear evidence of Beethoven's style, even though they are from the right period. Moreover, there is no sign of them among Beethoven's extensive sketches from 1819, nor any reference to such dances among the works he ever offered to publishers. There is also no indication of how the

[23] Ibid., p. 210. See Clive, *Beethoven and his World*, p. 207.
[24] See e.g. Arnold Schering, *Beethoven und die Dichtung* (Berlin: Junker & Dünnhaupt, 1936).
[25] Schindler, ed. MacArdle, *Beethoven*, p. 229.
[26] Ibid., p. 146.

music could have been transmitted from a Mödling band leader to Leipzig. Thus Schindler's account is presumably fictitious, and the set of eleven so-called 'Mödling' Dances spurious.

Several other works that have nothing to do with Beethoven have been wrongly attributed to him. One is a symphony in C, sometimes known as his 'Jena' Symphony or *Jugendsymphonie*, a supposedly early work that was in reality composed by Friedrich Witt. A pair of two-movement sonatinas in G and F that have become quite well known were at one time thought to be identifiable with two pieces sold at the auction of Beethoven's property in 1827; but it now appears that they were first published around 1807 by a publisher who had no known connection with Beethoven, and they are generally regarded as doubtful or spurious. Another spurious work is a funeral march in F minor, which can still be heard at war-memorial services in London on Remembrance Day – and still attributed to Beethoven. It was actually composed by Johann Heinrich Walch (1776–1855).[27]

In contrast to works incorrectly added to Beethoven's work-list, several that he wrote are sometimes completely ignored. Most conspicuously, it is generally stated that he composed thirty-two piano sonatas, a total that ignores three early works (WoO 47). There are even some books devoted specifically to his piano sonatas where these three works receive not a single mention. Elsewhere they have been referred to as sonatinas, but they are full-scale three-movement sonatas, and there is no justification for excluding them from editions or recordings of Beethoven's 'complete' piano sonatas, as is frequently done.[28] Since they were composed by Beethoven for the piano and published by him with the title 'Sonatas', what more could possibly be required in order to qualify as 'Beethoven piano sonatas'? His early concertos are often similarly ignored: there is a book by Antony Hopkins entitled *The Seven Concertos of Beethoven*.[29] Here there is slightly more justification for discounting the early ones, of which at least four were composed, since they survive only incomplete; but the total of only seven excludes all four. Other works often ignored include his folksong settings, which are sometimes referred to as mere 'arrangements', as if Beethoven did little more than change their scoring. And even when they are mentioned, their total number is often given incorrectly, with different accounts indicating such widely differing totals as 'nearly 130', 'about 150', 155, 164, 168, 171, 180, 187 and 190.[30] Actually there are precisely 179 of them.

---

[27] Georg Kinsky (completed Hans Halm), *Das Werk Beethovens: Thematisch-bibliographisches Verzeichnis seiner sämtlichen vollendeten Kompositionen* (Munich: Henle, 1955), Anh. 1, 5, and 13.

[28] The present writer's edition of *The 35 Piano Sonatas* (London: ABRSM, 2007) is one of the few to include these three sonatas.

[29] Antony Hopkins, *The Seven Concertos of Beethoven* (Aldershot: Scolar, 1996).

[30] See Cooper, *Beethoven's Folksong Settings*, p. 5.

The folksong settings and early piano sonatas are not the only works to have been devalued by being wrongly classified (as arrangements and sonatinas respectively). Beethoven's two one-act singspiels of 1811 – *Die Ruinen von Athen* (The Ruins of Athens) and *König Stephan* (King Stephen) – are often described as 'incidental music'. As in most singspiels, there is some spoken dialogue, which presumably gave rise to the wrong categorization; but the music is certainly not merely 'incidental'. It includes arias, grand choruses, and occasional melodrama (spoken dialogue with musical accompaniment) or recitative in which important elements of the action take place, and the works could even be classed as short operas. Without the music the spoken passages would fall to pieces, which is not the case with the truly incidental music for *Egmont*.

Many more anecdotes exist about Beethoven that are either wholly or partly fictitious, and several more compositions have been misattributed to him in the past. Other myths have arisen through scholarly error, or through unjustified speculation that, like Beethoven's 'fortresses' and Schering's poetic explanations, is all too easily presented or accepted as fact. The problem with all these myths, whether about Beethoven's life or his actual compositions, is that once they are in circulation they can never be completely removed.

Beethoven's place in history

Finally, let us address the myth of the historical position of Beethoven as 'the man who freed music' (the title of a book on Beethoven by R. H. Schauffler), breaking all the musical conventions of the time through not having to please a patron. In his music he was indeed constantly seeking to push the boundaries to their limits, but he was careful not to break with the past by contravening fundamental aesthetic principles – notably a devotion to a combination of 'the surprising and the beautiful', which he once stated to be the ideal.[31] Any suggestion that he was the first freelance composer able to live independently of patronage is also a myth. One cannot accept François Mai's claims that Beethoven refused many offers to become a Kapellmeister (music director) and was 'the world's first free-enterprise composer'.[32] As has been seen, he actually accepted an offer to become a Kapellmeister at Kassel in 1809, but was then induced to remain in Vienna by a better offer; and as late as 1822 he intended to apply for the post of imperial and royal chamber composer on the death of the previous incumbent until he was told that the position had been abolished. Moreover, although he did not work for an individual patron in Vienna, he was supported by several very generous ones. In addition, he was certainly

---

[31] A-1209; BB-1703.
[32] Mai, *Diagnosing Genius*, p. 6.

not the first free-enterprise composer; notable forerunners include Handel and Clementi.

Nevertheless these myths about Beethoven's historical position, like many myths, contain more than a grain of truth, for he does represent the beginning of a fundamentally changed perception of the role of the composer in society. Whereas music and its creation had in medieval times been regarded chiefly as an adjunct to other activities – usually worship, dancing, or narration – during the seventeenth and eighteenth centuries the rise of instrumental music lent it a certain autonomy as an independent activity. At the same time, however, perception of the value of music declined: it was no longer considered so much a reflection of divine glory as a mere harmless luxury, and of no real use on its own. But in the nineteenth century, attitudes to music changed again, and it now became the noblest and purest of the arts: noble through its ability to explore the inexpressible, the sublime, the subjective experience, yet pure through possessing no necessity to relate to anything outside itself, unlike, say, painting or literature. Although this change was partly due to evolving perceptions resulting from the Romantic movement, it was Beethoven who gave these ideas substance, since writers who wished to adopt them could invariably call on his music for their support. Thus Beethoven became the embodiment of the Romantic artist – a visionary figure who could not only create great and lasting works of art but even see into the future and write music appropriate for it. 'He writes for posterity' was a common complaint among his contemporaries, especially those who found his music difficult to fathom.

The idea of a musical composition as an enduring and historic artwork, fit for a museum or art gallery, found concrete expression as early as 1817, in the first edition of Beethoven's Piano Sonata Op. 101 in A major. This sonata was published as the first work in a new series entitled Museum für Klaviermusik (Museum for Piano Music), in which the publisher Sigmund Anton Steiner asserted that only compositions of recognized worth would be included. 'In this way we hope to found not just an ephemeral work but a *Repertory for Longer Time*, which must itself be of value in the history of our art.' These attitudes, new at the time, have become thoroughly embedded in our culture. Serious composers of today are still seen as creators of artworks of lasting value. That Beethoven could almost single-handedly produce such a profound change in cultural attitudes to music, by composing a body of works that self-evidently are first and foremost great art, is perhaps the most extraordinary achievement of a truly extraordinary life.

Bibliography of Literature Cited

ABBREVIATIONS

A-   Letter no. in Anderson (trans. and ed.), *The Letters of Beethoven* (see below).
Alb-   Item no. in Theodore Albrecht (trans. and ed.), *Letters to Beethoven and Other Correspondence*, 3 vols (Lincoln, NE: University of Nebraska Press, 1996).
BB-   Item no. in Sieghard Brandenburg (ed.), *Ludwig van Beethoven: Briefwechsel Gesamtausgabe*, 7 vols (Munich: Henle, 1996–8).
BKh   Karl-Heinz Köhler and others (eds.), *Ludwig van Beethovens Konversationshefte*, 11 vols to date (Leipzig: Deutscher Verlag für Musik, 1968–2001).
Hess   Item no. in James F. Green (trans. and ed.), *The New Hess Catalog of Beethoven's Works* (West Newbury, VT: Vance Brook, 2003; originally published as Willy Hess, *Verzeichnis der nicht in der Gesamtausgabe veröffentlichten Werke Ludwig van Beethovens*, Wiesbaden: Breitfkopf & Härtel, 1957).
T-   Item no. in Solomon, 'Beethoven's Tagebuch' (see below).
TF   *Thayer's Life of Beethoven*, ed. Elliot Forbes (Princeton: Princeton University Press, 2nd edn, 1967).
TDR   Alexander Wheelock Thayer (rev. Hermann Deiters and Hugo Riemann), *Ludwig van Beethovens Leben*, 5 vols (Leipzig: Breitkopf & Härtel, 1907–23).
WoO   Item no. in Kinsky, *Das Werk Beethovens* (see below).
WR   Franz Wegeler and Ferdinand Ries, *Remembering Beethoven*, trans. Frederick Noonan (London: André Deutsch, 1988; originally published as *Biographische Notizen über Ludwig van Beethoven*, Koblenz, 1838).

OTHER LITERATURE

Altman, Gail, *Beethoven: A Man of his Word* (Tallahassee, FL: Anubian Press, 1996).
Anderson, Emily (trans. and ed.), *The Letters of Beethoven*, 3 vols (London: Macmillan, 1961).
Baker, Nancy Kovaleff, and Thomas Christensen (eds.), *Aesthetics and the Art of Musical Composition in the German Enlightenment* (Cambridge: Cambridge University Press, 1995).
Beahrs, Virginia, ' "My Angel, my All, my Self" : A Literal Translation of Beethoven's Letter to the Immortal Beloved', *The Beethoven Newsletter*, 5 (1990), pp. 29, 34–9.
Biba, Otto (ed.), *Ludwig van Beethoven: Symphonie Nr. 3, Es-dur, op. 55, 'Eroica': Partitur-Manuskript (Beethovens Handexemplar): Vollständige Faksimile-Ausgabe in Originalformat* (Vienna: Gesellschaft der Musikfreunde, 1993).
Breuning, Gerhard von, *Memories of Beethoven*, trans. Henry Mins and Maynard Solomon, ed. Maynard Solomon (Cambridge: Cambridge University Press, 1992; originally published as *Aus dem Schwarzspanierhause: Erinnerungen an L. van Beethoven aus meiner Jugendzeit*, Vienna, 1874).
Busch-Weise, Dagmar von, 'Beethovens Jugendtagebuch', *Studien zur Musikwissenschaft*, 25 (1962), pp. 68–88.

Celeda, Jaroslav, 'Beethoven's "Immortal Beloved"', ed. Oldrich Pulkert, rev. Hans-Werner Küthen, trans. William Meredith, *The Beethoven Journal*, 15 (2000), pp. 2–18.

Clive, Peter, *Beethoven and his World: A Biographical Dictionary* (Oxford: Oxford University Press, 2001).

Cooper, Barry, *Beethoven* (Oxford: Oxford University Press, 2000; 2nd edn, New York, 2008).

——, *Beethoven and the Creative Process* (Oxford: Clarendon Press, 1990).

——, 'Beethoven and the Double Bar', *Music & Letters*, 88 (2007), pp. 458–83.

——, *Beethoven's Folksong Settings* (Oxford: Clarendon Press, 1994).

——, 'Beethoven's Revisions to *Für Elise*', *The Musical Times*, 125 (1984), pp. 561–3.

——, 'Beethoven's Revisions to his Fourth Piano Concerto', in Robin Stowell (ed.), *Performing Beethoven* (Cambridge: Cambridge University Press, 1994), pp. 23–48.

——, 'Beethoven's Oratorio and the Heiligenstadt Testament', *The Beethoven Journal*, 10 (1995), pp. 19–24.

——, 'The Clementi–Beethoven Contract of 1807: A Reinvestigation', in Roberto Illiano, Luca Sala, and Massimiliano Sala (eds.), *Muzio Clementi: Studies and Prospects* (Bologna: Ut Orpheus, 2002), pp. 337–53.

——, 'The Composition of "Und spür' ich" in Beethoven's *Fidelio*', *The Music Review*, 47 (1986–7), pp. 231–7.

——, 'Schindler and the *Pastoral* Symphony', *The Beethoven Newsletter*, 8 (1993), pp. 2–6.

——, 'The Two – or Two Dozen – Finales for Beethoven's Quartet Opus 130', *Ad Parnassum*, 8/16 (Oct. 2010), pp. 7–52.

——(ed.), *The Beethoven Compendium* (London: Thames & Hudson, 1991).

Czerny, Carl, *On the Proper Performance of All Beethoven's Works for the Piano*, ed. Paul Badura-Skoda (Vienna: Universal Edition, 1970).

Davies, Peter J., *Beethoven in Person: His Illnesses, Deafness, and Death* (Westport, CT: Greenwood, 2001).

DeNora, Tia, *Beethoven and the Construction of Genius: Musical Politics in Vienna, 1792–1803* (Berkeley: University of California Press, 1995).

Drabkin, William, *Beethoven: Missa solemnis* (Cambridge: Cambridge University Press, 1991).

Ealy, George Thomas, 'Of Ear Trumpets and a Resonance Plate: Early Hearing Aids and Beethoven's Hearing Perception', *19th-Century Music*, 17 (1993–4), pp. 262–73.

Eisinger, Josef, 'Was Beethoven Lead-Poisoned?', *The Beethoven Journal*, 23 (2008), pp. 15–17.

Gärtner, Heinz, *Constanze Mozart: After the Requiem*, trans. Reinhard G. Pauly (Portland, OR: Amadeus Press, 1991).

Gerber, Ernst Ludwig, *Historisch-biographisches Lexicon der Tonkünstler* (1790–1792), ed. Othmar Wessely (Graz: Akademische Druck- und Verlagsanstalt, 1977).

Hanson, Alice M., 'Incomes and Outgoings in the Vienna of Beethoven and Schubert', *Music & Letters*, 64 (1983), pp. 173–82.

Hopkins, Antony, *The Seven Concertos of Beethoven* (Aldershot: Scolar, 1996).

Howell, Standley, 'Beethoven's Maelzel Canon: Another Schindler Forgery?', *The Musical Times*, 120 (1979), pp. 987–90.

Johnson, Douglas, *Beethoven's Early Sketches in the 'Fischhof' Miscellany: Berlin: Autograph 28*, 2 vols (Ann Arbor, MI: UMI, 1980).

Johnson, Douglas (ed.), *The Beethoven Sketchbooks* (Oxford: Clarendon Press, 1985).

Jones, David Wyn, 'The *Missa solemnis* Premiere: First Rites', *The Musical Times*, 139 (Autumn 1998), pp. 25–8.

Kinsky, Georg (completed Hans Halm), *Das Werk Beethovens: Thematisch-bibliographisches Verzeichnis seiner sämtlicher vollendeten Kompositionen* (Munich: Henle, 1955).

Klein, Hans-Günter, *Ludwig van Beethoven: Autographe und Abschriften*, Staatsbibliothek Preussischer Kulturbesitz: Kataloge der Musikabteilung, I/2 (Berlin: Merseburger, 1975).

Kopitz, Klaus Martin, 'Beethoven as a Composer for the Orphica: A New Source for WoO 51', *The Beethoven Journal*, 22 (2007), pp. 25–30 (see also correspondence, ibid., 23 (2008), p. 47).

Landon, H. C. Robbins, *Beethoven: A Documentary Study* (London: Thames & Hudson, 1970).

Lockwood, Lewis, 'The Autograph of the First Movement of Beethoven's Sonata for Violoncello and Pianoforte, Opus 69', *The Music Forum*, 2 (1970), pp. 1–109.

——, *Beethoven: The Music and the Life* (New York: Norton, 2003).

Lund, Susan, *Raptus: A Novel about Beethoven* (Melbourn, Herts.: Melstamps, 1995).

Mai, François Martin, *Diagnosing Genius: The Life and Death of Beethoven* (Montreal: McGill-Queen's University Press, 2007).

Marston, Nicholas, 'In the "Twilight Zone": Beethoven's Unfinished Piano Trio in F minor', *Journal of the Royal Musical Association*, 131 (206), pp. 227–86.

Nottebohm, Gustav, *Beethoven's Studien* (Leipzig and Winterthur: Peters, 1873).

Reid, Paul, *The Beethoven Song Companion* (Manchester: Manchester University Press, 2007).

Reiter, Christian, 'The Causes of Beethoven's Death and his Locks of Hair: A Forensic-Toxicological Investigation', trans. Michael Lorenz, *The Beethoven Journal*, 22 (2007), pp. 2–5 (see also correspondence, ibid., pp. 124–5).

Rumph, Stephen, *Beethoven after Napoleon* (Berkeley and Los Angeles: University of California Press, 2004).

Schering, Arnold, *Beethoven und die Dichtung* (Berlin: Junker & Dünnhaupt, 1936).

Schindler, Anton, *Beethoven as I Knew Him*, trans. Constance Jolly, ed. Donald MacArdle (London: Faber & Faber, 1966; originally published as *Biographie von Ludwig van Beethoven*, 3rd edn, Münster, 1860).

Schlosser, Johann Aloys, *Beethoven: The First Biography [1827]*, trans. Reinhard G. Pauly, ed. Barry Cooper (Portland, OR: Amadeus, 1996; originally published as *Ludwig van Beethoven: Eine Biographie desselben, verbunden mit Urtheilen über seine Werke*, Prague, 1828 [Sept. 1827]).

Schmidt-Görg, Joseph (ed.), *Des Bonner Bäckermeisters Gottfried Fischer Aufzeichnungen über Beethovens Jugend* (Bonn: Beethovenhaus, 1971).

Sisman, Elaine (ed.), *Haydn and his World* (Princeton, NJ: Princeton University Press, 1997).

Sloane, Donald F., 'A Multiple-Choice Quiz on the Historical Accuracy of Bernard Rose's *Immortal Beloved*', *The Beethoven Journal*, 10 (1995), pp. 30–1.

Solomon, Maynard, *Beethoven* (New York: Schirmer, 1977).

——, *Beethoven Essays* (Cambridge, MA: Harvard University Press, 1988).

——, 'Beethoven's Tagebuch of 1812–1818', in Alan Tyson (ed.), *Beethoven Studies 3* (Cambridge: Cambridge University Press, 1982), pp. 193–288.

——, 'Economic Circumstances of the Beethoven Household in Bonn', *Journal of the American Musicological Society*, 50 (1997), pp. 331–51.

Sonneck, O. G. (ed.), *Beethoven: Impressions by his Contemporaries* (New York: Schirmer, 1926; reprinted New York: Dover, 1967).

Stanley, Glenn, (ed.), *The Cambridge Companion to Beethoven* (Cambridge: Cambridge University Press, 2000).

Steblin, Rita, '"A dear, enchanting girl who loves me and whom I love": New Facts about Beethoven's Beloved Pupil Julie Guicciardi', *Bonner Beethoven-Studien*, 8 (2009), pp. 89–152.

Suchet, John, *The Last Master … A Fictional Biography of Ludwig van Beethoven*, 3 vols (London: Little, Brown, 1996–8).

Tellenbach, Marie-Elisabeth, *Beethoven und seine 'unsterbliche Geliebte' Josephine Brunswick* (Zurich: Atlantis, 1983).

——, 'Künstler und Ständegesellschaft um 1800: Die Rolle der Vormundschaftsgesetze in Beethovens Beziehung zu Josephine Gräfin Deym', *Vierteljahrschrift für Sozial- und Wirtschaftsgeschichte*, 75 (1988), pp. 253–63.

Tyson, Alan, 'The Problem of Beethoven's "First" *Leonore* Overture', *Journal of the American Musicological Society*, 28 (1975), pp. 292–334.

Van der Zanden, Jos, 'Letter to the Editor', *The Beethoven Journal*, 21 (2006), p. 47.

Walden, Edward, *Beethoven's Immortal Beloved: Solving the Mystery* (Lanham, MD: Scarecrow Press, 2011).

Webster, James, 'The Falling-Out between Haydn and Beethoven: The Evidence of the Sources', in Lewis Lockwood and Phyllis Benjamin (eds.), *Beethoven Essays: Studies in Honor of Elliot Forbes* (Cambridge, MA: Harvard University Press, 1984), pp. 3–45.

WEBSITES:

www.beethoven-haus-bonn.de (Beethoven-Haus site, with much information about Beethoven's works; also includes a digital archive with online reproduction of all Beethoven manuscripts and much printed music held at the Beethoven-Archiv in Bonn; last accessed 28 February 2013).

www.sjsu.edu/beethoven (Beethoven Center site at San Jose State University, California; includes online access to the Beethoven Bibliography Database, the most comprehensive Beethoven bibliography available; last accessed 28 February 2013).

Index

works

Canons
  Kühl nicht lau (WoO 191), 129
  O Tobias (WoO 182), 122
  Ta ta ta (WoO 162: spurious), 154

Chamber music
(i) with wind
  Clarinet Trio (Op. 11), 47, 52, 81
  Horn Sonata (Op. 17), 52, 81
  Octet (Op. 103), 9, 40
  Quintet (Op. 16), 45–6
  Quintet (Hess 19), 40–1
  Septet (Op. 20), 50, 81
  Trio (WoO 37), 15, 80–1
  Variations for flute and piano (Opp. 105
    and 107), 9, 121
(ii) for piano and strings, 4
  Cello Sonata in F (Op. 5 No. 1), 45
  Cello Sonata in G minor (Op. 5 No. 2),
    45
  Cello Sonata in A (Op. 69), 32–4
  Cello Sonata in C (Op. 102 No. 1), 81,
    104
  Cello Sonata in D (Op. 102 No. 2), 81, 104
  4 mandolin pieces (WoO 43–4), 45, 80
  Quartet in E flat (WoO 36 No. 1), 15
  Quartet in D (WoO 36 No. 2), 15
  Quartet in C (WoO 36 No. 3), 15
  Trio in E flat (Op. 1 No. 1), 9, 39, 42–5
  Trio in G (Op. 1 No. 2), 9, 39, 42–5
  Trio in C minor (Op. 1 No. 3), 9, 39, 42–5
  Trio in D (Op. 70 No. 1), 81
  Trio in E flat (Op. 70 No. 2), 81
  Trio in B flat ('Archduke', Op. 97), 6,
    97–8, 153
  Trio in B flat (WoO 39), 81, 89
  Variations for piano and cello ('Ein
    Mädchen oder Weibchen', Op. 66),
    25, 45
  Variations for piano and cello ('See the
    conqu'ring hero', WoO 45), 45, 80
  Variations for piano and violin ('Se vuol
    ballare', WoO 40), 40, 43, 80
  Violin Sonata in D (Op. 12 No. 1), 47
  Violin Sonata in A (Op. 12 No. 2), 47
  Violin Sonata in E flat (Op. 12 No. 3), 47
  Violin Sonata in G (Op. 96), 100
(iii) for strings alone, 4, 6
  Grosse Fuge for string quartet (Op. 133),
    28, 130–1
  Quartet in F (Op. 18 No. 1), 26, 48–9
  Quartet in G (Op. 18 No. 2), 26, 48–9
  Quartet in D (Op. 18 No. 3), 26, 48–9
  Quartet in C minor (Op. 18 No. 4), 26,
    48–9
  Quartet in A (Op. 18 No. 5), 26, 48–9
  Quartet in B flat (Op. 18 No. 6), 26, 48–9
  Quartet in F ('Razumovsky', Op. 59
    No. 1), 65, 75–6

Quartet in E minor ('Razumovsky',
    Op. 59 No. 2), 65, 75–6
Quartet in C ('Razumovsky', Op. 59
    No. 3), 63, 65, 75–6
Quartet in E flat ('Harp', Op. 74), 94
Quartet in F minor (*Serioso*, Op. 95), 97
Quartet in E flat (Op. 127), 5, 9, 27, 123,
    126–7, 130
Quartet in B flat (Op. 130), 5, 9, 27, 123,
    126–7, 129–31
Quartet in C sharp minor (Op. 131), 27,
    127, 130
Quartet in A minor (Op. 132), 5, 9, 27,
    123, 126–7, 130
Quartet in F (Op. 135), 27, 31, 130–1
Quintet in E flat (Op. 4), 44
Serenade for string trio (Op. 8), 47
Trio in E flat (Op. 3), 44
3 trios (Op. 9), 47

Choral Music
  'Bundeslied' (Op. 122), 123
  Cantata on Joseph II, 18–19
  Cantata on Leopold II, 18–19
  Choral Fantasia, 78–9
  Christus am Oelberge (Christ on the
    Mount of Olives), 64–5, 67–9, 72
  Elegischer Gesang (Elegiac Song), 81
  Gesang der Mönche (Song of the Monks),
    46
  Der glorreiche Augenblick (The Glorious
    Moment), 103
  Hochzeitslied (Wedding Song), 81
  Italian partsongs (WoO 99), 67
  Mass in C, 77–8, 81
  Meerestille und glückliche Fahrt (Calm Sea
    and Prosperous Voyage), 100
  Missa solemnis, 6, 9, 33–4, 113, 119–23,
    125, 136, 155
  'Opferlied' (Op. 121b), 123
  'Pange lingua', 120

Counterpoint exercises, 40, 42

Dance music
  12 Contredanses (WoO 14), 34–5, 53
  12 German Dances (WoO 8), 44
  6 German Dances (WoO 42), 80
  12 Minuets (WoO 7), 44
  6 Minuets (WoO 10), 44
  11 'Mödling' Dances (WoO 17:
    spurious), 155–6

Folksong settings, 9, 82, 91, 94–6, 105,
    156–57
  Scottish Airs (Op. 108), 121

Marches
  3 Marches (WoO 18–20), 123

Orchestral Music
  'Jena' Symphony (spurious), 156
  Oboe Concerto (Hess 12), 40–1, 49